Chapter 1: Gender Equality Today

Chapter 2: Obstacles to Equality

Introduction

Gender Equality is Volume 432 in the **issues** series. The aim of the series is to offer current, diverse information about important issues in our world, from a UK perspective.

About Gender Equality

With gender equality centuries away, there is still a lot to do to improve equality. This book looks at the big issues that continue to be debated around the topic, such as the gender pay gap, the chore gap and the harmful stereotypes affecting both females and males.

Our sources

Titles in the **issues** series are designed to function as educational resource books, providing a balanced overview of a specific subject.

The information in our books is comprised of facts, articles and opinions from many different sources, including:

- Newspaper reports and opinion pieces
- Website factsheets
- Magazine and journal articles
- Statistics and surveys
- Government reports
- Literature from special interest groups.

A note on critical evaluation

Because the information reprinted here is from a number of different sources, readers should bear in mind the origin of the text and whether the source is likely to have a particular bias when presenting information (or when conducting their research). It is hoped that, as you read about the many aspects of the issues explored in this book, you will critically evaluate the information presented.

It is important that you decide whether you are being presented with facts or opinions. Does the writer give a biased or unbiased report? If an opinion is being expressed, do you agree with the writer? Is there potential bias to the 'facts' or statistics behind an article?

Activities

Throughout this book, you will find a selection of assignments and activities designed to help you engage with the articles you have been reading and to explore your own opinions. Some tasks will take longer than others and there is a mixture of design, writing and research-based activities that you can complete alone or in a group.

Further research

At the end of each article we have listed its source and a website that you can visit if you would like to conduct your own research. Please remember to critically evaluate any sources that you consult and consider whether the information you are viewing is accurate and unbiased.

Issues Online

The **issues** series of books is complemented by our online resource, issuesonline.co.uk

On the Issues Online website you will find a wealth of information, covering over 70 topics, to support the PSHE and RSE curriculum.

Why Issues Online?

Researching a topic? Issues Online is the best place to start for...

Librarians

Issues Online is an essential tool for librarians: feel confident you are signposting safe, reliable, user-friendly online resources to students and teaching staff alike. We provide multi-user concurrent access, so no waiting around for another student to finish with a resource. Issues Online also provides FREE downloadable posters for your shelf/wall/table displays.

Teachers

Issues Online is an ideal resource for lesson planning, inspiring lively debate in class and setting lessons and homework tasks.

Our accessible, engaging content helps deepen students' knowledge, promotes critical thinking and develops independent learning skills.

Issues Online saves precious preparation time. We wade through the wealth of material on the internet to filter the best quality, most relevant and up-to-date information you need to start exploring a topic.

Our carefully selected, balanced content presents an overview and insight into each topic from a variety of sources and viewpoints.

Students

Issues Online is designed to support your studies in a broad range of topics, particularly social issues relevant to young people today.

Thousands of articles, statistics and infographs instantly available to help you with research and assignments.

With 24/7 access using the powerful Algolia search system, you can find relevant information quickly, easily and safely anytime from your laptop, tablet or smartphone, in class or at home.

Visit issuesonline.co.uk to find out more!

Gender gap: these are the world's most gender-equal countries

- It will take 132 years to reach gender parity, according to the World Economic Forum's Global Gender Gap Report 2022 – with only 68% of the gender gap closed.

- Iceland tops the rankings and is the only economy to have closed more than 90% of its gap.

- The top 10 economies have all closed more than 80% of their gender gap.

Iceland has once again been named the most gender equal country, topping the World Economic Forum's Global Gender Gap Report 2022.

The Nordic country has closed more than 90% of its gender gap – and tops the ranking for the 12th year in a row, out of a total of 146 economies in the 2022 Global Gender Gap Index.

Global gender gap index 2022 – Global, top 10

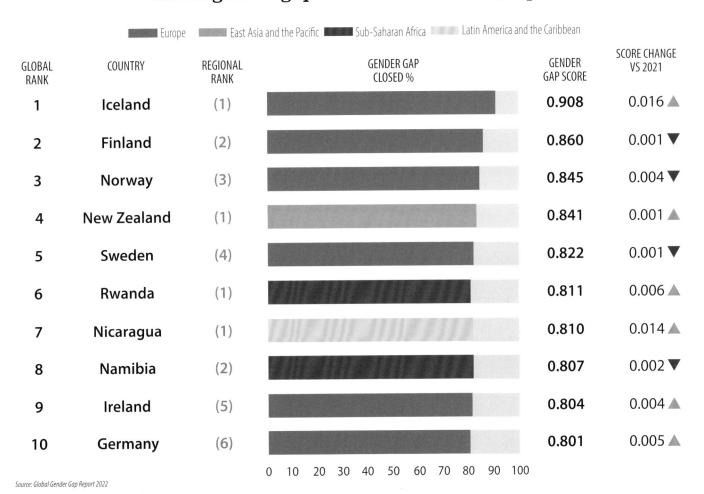

Europe   East Asia and the Pacific   Sub-Saharan Africa   Latin America and the Caribbean

GLOBAL RANK	COUNTRY	REGIONAL RANK	GENDER GAP CLOSED %	GENDER GAP SCORE	SCORE CHANGE VS 2021
1	Iceland	(1)		0.908	0.016 ▲
2	Finland	(2)		0.860	0.001 ▼
3	Norway	(3)		0.845	0.004 ▼
4	New Zealand	(1)		0.841	0.001 ▲
5	Sweden	(4)		0.822	0.001 ▼
6	Rwanda	(1)		0.811	0.006 ▲
7	Nicaragua	(1)		0.810	0.014 ▲
8	Namibia	(2)		0.807	0.002 ▼
9	Ireland	(5)		0.804	0.004 ▲
10	Germany	(6)		0.801	0.005 ▲

0 10 20 30 40 50 60 70 80 90 100

Source: Global Gender Gap Report 2022

Iceland's near neighbours Finland, Norway and Sweden dominate the top five, while only four countries in the top 10 are outside Europe: New Zealand (4th), Rwanda (6th), Nicaragua (7th) and Namibia (8th).

The top five are unchanged from last year, but Lithuania and Switzerland have dropped out of the top 10, with Nicaragua and Germany taking their places.

Since 2006, the Global Gender Gap Index has measured the world's progress towards gender parity across four key dimensions: Economic Participation and Opportunity, Educational Attainment, Health and Survival, and Political Empowerment.

At a global level, only 68.1% of the gender gap has been closed, meaning it will take another 132 years to reach gender parity. This is a slight improvement from last year, but three decades longer than the situation in 2020, before the impacts of COVID-19 on gender equality.

Countries with the least gender gap in 2022

Here's what you need to know about the top 10 economies:

1. Iceland

Iceland has almost entirely closed its gender gap in Educational Attainment, with a score of 0.993, where 1 means equality has been reached. While only 22% of the global gender gap in Political Empowerment has been closed, Iceland tops the entire Index in this dimension, due to having a higher share of women as head of state over the past 50 years and a higher share of women in parliament than other countries.

A fair sharing of unpaid work has been instrumental to Iceland's progress, Joeli Brearley, author of *The Motherhood Penalty*, told the World Economic Forum: 'When 90% of women went on strike over this in the 1970s, it showed men there is value in this work, they cannot do their jobs without it. That was the big shift for Iceland in terms of gender equality.'

2. Finland

Finland has achieved full parity in Educational Attainment and near parity (0.97) in the Health and Survival subindex. But its 2022 score in Economic Participation and Opportunity (0.789) is lower than for 2021 (0.806) due to a drop in parity for labour force participation, a fall in both men's and women's estimated earned income, and a decline in gender parity in wage equality.

3. Norway

At 0.845, Norway's score is slightly lower than its highest achieved in 2021. Educational Attainment is Norway's highest subindex score at near full parity (0.989). In Economic Participation and Opportunity, the country's score of 0.765 marks a decrease of 3% from a year earlier, slipping to levels Norway registered back in 2007. This year's numbers reflect lower levels of women participating in the workforce, and holding posts as legislators, senior officials and managers.

4. New Zealand

New Zealand has achieved parity across the board in the Education category. In Health and Survival, it has improved its ranking in healthy life expectancy. The level of parity the country reached this year in the Economic subindex is lower than last year, as the rate at which women participate in the workforce decreased, although wage equality for similar work increased. In the Political Empowerment subindex, New Zealand improved its score from last year by 0.03, as its share of female leadership at head-of-state level increased.

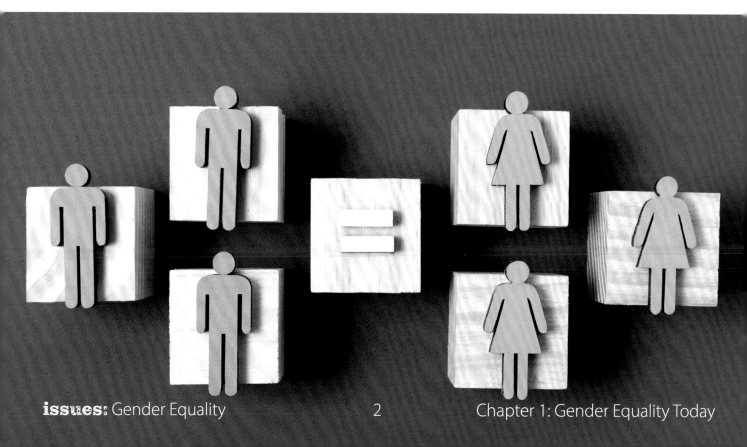

5. Sweden

Sweden has closed the gender gap on Educational Attainment and its second-highest score is in the Health and Survival subindex (0.963), where it holds on to the gains made in 2021. It comes first for Economic Participation and Opportunity in the region, with a high level of female workforce participation, parity in the participation of women in professional and technical roles, and a level of parity in estimated earned income higher than 137 other countries.

6. Rwanda

Rwanda has featured in the top 10 every year since it was first included in the Index in 2014 – and this year it has climbed one place in the rankings, as well as leading Sub- Saharan Africa. Its highest subindex scores are in Educational Attainment and Health and Survival (0.96 and 0.974, respectively). It has reduced the gender gap in tertiary education by 2.9% and maintained parity in compulsory education.

In Economic Participation and Opportunity, Rwanda is one of three economies that registered parity in labour force participation in 2022 (alongside Sierra Leone and Burundi). In Political Empowerment, the country also recorded parity at ministerial and parliamentary levels.

7. Nicaragua

Progress since 2021 sees Nicaragua move up five places in 2022 to 7th position. It has closed the gap in the Educational Attainment subindex, across all its indicators. In the Political Empowerment subindex, Nicaragua remained in 5th spot, with continued parity in ministerial positions from 2021. It has raised its score for parliamentary parity from 0.938 last year to 1.

But its gender gaps have widened in Economic Participation and Opportunity since 2017. This year, the gaps are evident in women's labour force participation and in wage equality. However, Nicaragua has maintained 2021 levels of women's participation in professional, technical roles, and as legislators, officials and senior managers. Equality on estimated earned income also increased, from 0.456 to 0.682.

8. Namibia

Namibia has dropped two places since last year. Its performance in the Health and Survival subindex has

Key Facts

- According to the World Economic Forum Global Gender Gap Report 2022, it will take 132 years to reach gender parity.

- Iceland has topped the rankings as the most gender equal country for 12 years in a row.

- The top 10 economies have all closed more than 80% of their gender gap.

Research

In pairs, look online at the current Global Gender Gap Report from the World Economic Forum. Can you find where the UK ranks in the each of the following categories:

- Economic participation and opportunity
- Educational attainment
- Health and survival
- Political empowerment

Where does the UK rank overall? Why do you think the UK isn't in the top 10? Discuss with your research partner and share your thoughts with the rest of the class.

remained unchanged since 2014, but it reported lower levels of parity in three Economic Participation and Opportunity indicators than in 2021: women's labour force participation (-0.014), wage equality (-0.017) and estimated earned income (-0.005).

Although it reported parity across all levels of education and a high literacy score (0.998), Namibia's ranking in the Educational Attainment subindex has not gained ground since slipping from parity in 2016. In the Political Empowerment pillar, the only change in 2022 was a small reduction of the gender gap score for women in ministerial positions (-0.001).

9. Ireland

Ireland remains in 9th place, but it has recovered ground lost since posting its highest score in 2016 (0.806). It closed the gap in the Educational Attainment subindex, and its overall Economic Participation score rose by 0.013 thanks to continued parity in women's participation as professional and technical workers, and by a reduction of gender gaps in estimated earned income, wage equality, and the participation of legislators, senior officials, and managers. But these improvements are countered by a drop of 0.026 in women's labour force participation.

10. Germany

Germany's 2022 score is its highest ever and it returns to the top 10 this year, having ranked between 10 and 14 since 2008. It ranks highest in Political Empowerment, which is also the subindex where it has the highest level of improvement. Its score of 0.55 is higher than 94% of countries in the Index. It maintains high levels of parity in Educational Attainment, but has lower scores across indicators in Economic Participation and Opportunity compared with 2021.

13 July 2022

www.weforum.org

INTERNATIONAL
Women's Day

In an article for FE News (a further education focused news website) in January 2023, the chief of learning at the Micro:Bit Educational Foundation, Magda Wood, warned that STEM was not being 'presented as a safe space' for girls and this prevented girls from studying the subjects. She argued that much of what the government could do to 'solve STEM's diversity issue' was dependent on 'what happens in the classroom'. Therefore, she called on the government to categorise all STEM subjects as 'core subjects' and give them the same recognition and investment of resources as other subjects. Additionally, she said that the government needed to 'show some initiative' to change societal views on STEM professions by presenting the opportunities to young people that STEM subjects could have. She argued that this would 'make sure young girls know it is a space for them'.

In November 2021, the Institute of Engineering and Technology published an open letter it had sent to the then prime minister, Boris Johnson, calling on the government to address a skills gap within UK workforces. In the letter, the 167 cosignatories warned that there was a shortfall of 173,000 workers in the STEM sector, estimated to cost the economy £1.5bn per year. They argued that 'future skills need addressing now' and that the solution 'lies in education'. They called on the government to collaborate with STEM education supporters, academia and industry to provide teachers 'with the tools they need to showcase that science, design and technology and maths all have vital elements of engineering within them' and to proactively encourage the teaching of engineering in our primary schools'.

In the same month, the House of Commons Science and Technology Committee launched its inquiry into diversity and inclusion in STEM. On the inquiry webpage, the committee stated that there was 'evidence to suggest' that women, amongst other groups, were underrepresented in education, training and employment related to STEM. The committee said it would be exploring how the government, funding bodies, industry and academia could work to address issues identified during the inquiry and has run a number of evidence sessions. As of February 2023, the committee has not published a report of its findings.

In June 2020, the All Party Parliamentary Group (APPG) on Diversity and Inclusion in STEM published a report into equity in STEM education. The APPG stated that initiatives to attract more girls into physics and computing had received government support which was 'welcome' but was 'yet to make a significant difference in these subjects at GCSE or A level'. The APPG also made several recommendations for the government, including calling for STEM-specific teaching to be strengthened and a 'more joined-up approach' to tackle the causes of inequity in STEM education.

2.3 Worldwide

Successive Conservative governments have also taken measures to try to remove the barriers to girls' education and promote gender equality in education in developing countries. The charity UNICEF states that there are many barriers to girls' education, which vary amongst countries and communities. Barriers include discrimination based on gender stereotypes in wider communities and poorer families often favouring boys when investing in education.

In February 2023, the government announced £80mn of funding over the next four years (2023 to 2026) to support the work of Education Cannot Wait, which is the UN's global fund for education in emergencies. The government said that the funding would go towards providing safe learning spaces, teaching materials and psychological and social support to children and adolescents affected by war, disaster and displacement. In September 2022, the government launched the 'Commitment to action on foundational learning' initiative alongside several organisations, including UNICEF and the World Bank. The initiative sought to commit countries to act to secure foundation learning for all children and ensure that children can read, do basic mathematics and build socio-emotional skills by the age of 10. In September 2022, the government reported that the initiative had been endorsed by Bulgaria, Egypt and Sierra Leone.

To mark IWD in March 2022, the government and businesses from the private sector, including Microsoft and Unilever, launched a global programme called the 'Girls' education skills partnership'. The partnership sought to improve girls' access to education in developing countries. Funds were contributed by the government and private sector (£9 million and £11 million, respectively). Funding would also be used towards expanding Generation Unlimited's 'Passport to earning' platform, which would provide girls with free, certified education and skills training, which could be used to support future employment. Generation Unlimited is a public-private youth partnership launched by the UN secretary-general in 2018. The countries identified for the platform included Bangladesh, Nigeria and Pakistan.

In July 2021, the government co-hosted the Global Education Summit alongside the Kenyan government, which raised £2.9bn for the Global Partnership for Education (GPE). The GPE is a multilateral partnership aiming to improve education in developing countries. The partnership also seeks to increase the number of girls who complete primary and secondary education. At the summit, the government announced £430mn of new funding would go towards the partnership.

In May 2021, the then government published the 'girls' education action plan'. The plan detailed measures to help meet the G7's targets for 2026 of getting 40 million more girls into school and 20 million more girls reading by 10 years old. This included rolling out new initiatives in Africa and Asia focused on 'overcoming the barriers that marginalised girls face during adolescence' and providing catch-up programmes to 'get girls on track with their learning'. Alongside the publication of the action plan, the government announced £55mn of funding to create the 'What Works Hub for Global Education' programme. The aim of the programme would be to advise governments in Africa and Asia on reforming school systems and supporting female enrolment in education.

2.4 How effective has recent government policy been in supporting girls' education in developing countries?

Although the UK aid-funded education programmes in developing countries have been praised, barriers remain.

In April 2022, the Independent Commission for Aid Impact (ICAI) published its report following a review of UK aid-funded education programming in developing countries. ICAI stated that it found education programmes funded by UK aid to be 'ambitious', 'mainly well implemented' and 'relevant to the needs of highly marginalised children, particularly hard-to-reach girls'. Despite this, ICAI argued that barriers remained for improving the quality of education and learning in these countries. Some of this was because of attitudes to gender roles and inadequate menstrual hygiene management facilities in schools. ICAI also noted that a quarter of programmes with activities to support girls did not meet the expectations of the former Department for International Development, now the Foreign, Commonwealth and Development Office (FCDO), in this area. Therefore, ICAI made several recommendations, including calling on the FCDO to ensure that all its aid towards education programmes 'maintains a consistent focus on girls' in its design and implementation.

The government published its response to the review in June 2022, accepting ICAI's recommendations. Specifically addressing the point that aid for education programmes needed to maintain a consistent focus on girls, the government stated that it had 'made progress' in this area but agreed there was 'still more to do'. It stated that it would measure its success by progress made by girls 'in the most challenging of circumstances', and that if they are 'thriving in education, then we will know we are making progress'.

27 February 2023

Key Facts

- The UN noted that 37% of women do not use the internet and that 259 million fewer women have access to the internet than men, despite accounting for nearly half of the world's population.

- The WEF has published an annual 'global gender gap report' since 2006, assessing progress across 146 countries.

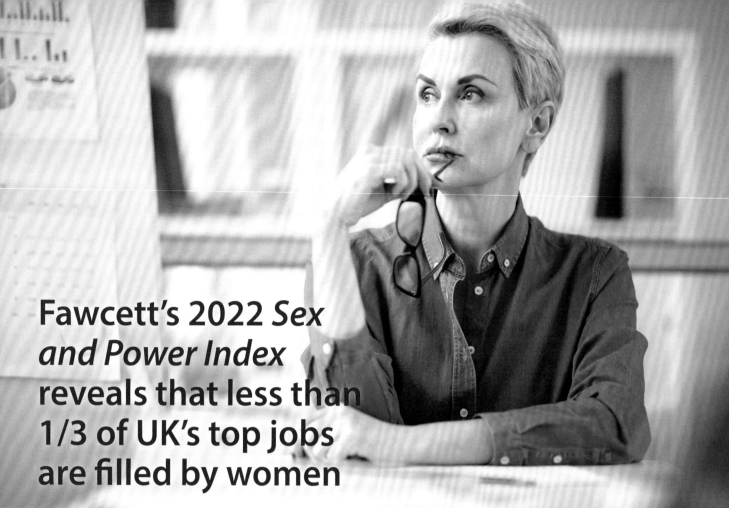

Fawcett's 2022 *Sex and Power Index* reveals that less than 1/3 of UK's top jobs are filled by women

The Fawcett Society is today publishing its 2022 *Sex and Power Index* – the biennial report which charts the progress towards equal representation for women in top jobs across the UK. Yet again, the report reveals the pace of change is glacial in the majority of sectors and shows that women are outnumbered by men 2:1 in positions of power.

The data also shows that women of colour are under-represented at the highest levels in many sectors and alarmingly, reveals that they are missing altogether from senior roles such as Supreme Court Justices, Metro Mayors, Police and Crime Commissioners and FTSE 100 chief executives.

While overall progress is far too slow, the report shows that women's representation has improved in a minority of key areas with the Scottish Parliament, London Assembly, Combined Authorities and Local Economic Partnerships (LEPs) having made solid progress towards equality since the last *Sex and Power Index* was published in 2020. This clearly shows that progress is possible and there are lessons to be learned in sectors such as sport. The sporting sector not only has very few women in leadership roles, but this year's *Sex and Power Index* has revealed a progressive decline in the number of female sport governing body chairs (15% in 2022 from 20% in 2020) and CEOs (19% in 2022 from 21% in 2020).

Jemima Olchawski, CEO, The Fawcett Society, said:

'The people who hold the top jobs in our society have enormous power to shape our democracy, culture and economy. Yet men continue to dominate most senior roles. That's not only bad for the women who miss out on opportunities to thrive, but it's bad for us all, as we miss out on women's talent, skills and perspectives.'

What is most alarming about today's data is that it shows an unacceptable lack of women of colour in senior positions. It is appalling that in 2022, women of colour are missing in leadership positions from some of our key institutions and organisations. Put simply, this gives the lie to the idea that we live in a meritocracy or a society of equal opportunity. Structures, culture and often individuals continue to create barriers that prevent women and women of colour in particular rising to the top. And we're all losing out as a result.

Too few women in positions of power is one of the causes of the gender pay gap and the complete lack of women of colour in top jobs in many sectors also feeds the ethnicity pay gap. It is essential that this Government introduces intersectional ethnicity pay gap reporting and gets to grips with inequalities in our society that hold back women of colour.

Dianne Greyson, Founder #EthnicityPayGap Campaign:

'The Ethnicity Pay Gap Campaign is renewing its calls on the Government to introduce mandatory ethnicity pay gap reporting. This is a key step in addressing structural barriers that stop women from ethnic backgrounds progressing into positions of power. Our recent research shows that Black women experience pay disparity based on their race and are significantly held back in their career progression because of structural racism. It also highlights the considerable mental and physical pressures placed upon Black women in the workplace.

We want to see companies eradicate the cultural and systemic practices that impact women from an ethnic background.'

Sex and Power 2022 shows:

- **Parliaments and Politics:** The last two Westminster elections have seen scant progress, the proportion of female MPs moving from 32% in 2017 to 34% at the 2019 election.

- **Business:** Women remain just 8% of FTSE 100 CEOs, and none are women of colour. Women hold 37.7% of non-executive directorships, but just 13.7% of executive directorships.

- **Education:** Women account for 65% of secondary school teachers, but only 40% of headteachers. Just 6% of those headteachers are women from ethnic minority backgrounds.

- **Media:** The proportion of women editing national newspapers has risen to 42%, whilst the number of female political editors remains low at 12%.

- **Cabinet:** The proportion of women in Cabinet has fallen back to just over a quarter (26%) and only 24% of Cabinet Committee positions are held by women

- **Local Government:** Women make up 35% of councillors across England, 22% of local council leaders, and 26% of Police and Crime Commissioners. There are now greater numbers of women on combined authority boards - 37%, and women make up 52% of London Assembly members.

- **Civil Service:** Of the 16 government departments run by permanent secretaries, six are run by women and none are run by women of colour. Women's representation among the Civil Service Board stands at 45% women.

- **The Law:** Women make up 27% of Court of Appeal judges and 30% of High Court judges. There are just two female Supreme Court Justices and no women of colour.

- **Sport:** On individual sport bodies, only three CEOs, out of 22 organisations, are women (14%) This is a sharp decline from the 2020 Sex and Power report where women made up 21% of chief executives. Of all-time Premier League clubs, women make up 5% of chief executives.

- **Health:** The number of women chairing NHS trusts is getting closer to parity at 41% and 45% of trusts have a female chief executive. Amanda Prichard has become the first female NHS England chief executive.

- **Civil Society:** Women represent one in three chief executives of the largest 100 charities by income at 36%. Our analysis of 22 professional bodies found that women made up 24% of chief executives and 48% of chairs.

Jemima continues:

'The pandemic has laid bare the deep-rooted inequalities across the UK. Yet it is women who have borne the brunt and often largely invisible from debate and excluded from decision-making. Women of colour, disabled women, young women and mothers have been at the sharpest end.

At the height of the pandemic only two out of 56 Government press briefings were led by a female politician and women were underrepresented across all covid-19 advisory groups. It begs the question then, what if more women were at the table and making key decisions, would women across our society have felt the impact of political decisions throughout the pandemic so severely?'

Women's representation in the COVID-19 crisis:

The Index shows that at the height of the pandemic, women were underrepresented across the Scientific Advisory Group for Emergencies (SAGE) and related subgroups:

- Scientific Advisory Group for Emergencies (SAGE) - 28%

- Scientific Pandemic Insights Group on Behaviours (SPI-B) - 39%

- Scientific Pandemic Influenza Group on Modelling (SPI-M) - 24%

- COVID-19 Clinical Information Network (CO-CIN) - 11%

- New and Emerging Respiratory Virus Threats Advisory Group (NERVTAG) - 20% Environmental Modelling Group (EMG) - 21%

- Joint Committee on Vaccination and Immunisation (JCVI) - 25%

The Fawcett Society continues to call on Government to ensure more women are at the decision-making table. As of November 2021, only 92 of the 274 (34%) people on our COVID-19 advisory boards are women.

Women's representation across all sectors is a vitally important step to advancing gender equality and, as research continues to show, it is good for business.

Fawcett's Sex & Power 2022 calls for change include:

- Targets set to increase the number of women in positions of power and actions plans put in place to ensure they are met.

- Improved Pay Gap Reporting – which includes intersectional ethnicity pay gap reporting, the threshold for reporting reduced to employers with 100+ employees, and publication of mandatory action plans.

- Action plans must be established by co-ordinating bodies in sectors where women of colour are missing from the top.

- Flexible working as default for all job roles, where it is reasonably possible.

21st January 2022

Fawcett's *2022 Sex & Power Index* can be found here: www.fawcettsociety. org.uk/sex- power-2022

The above information is reprinted with kind permission from The Fawcett Society.
© The Fawcett Society 2022

www.fawcettsociety.org.uk

UK launches gender equality plan but critics call funding a 'drop in the ocean'

Foreign secretary's new strategy branded 'meaningless' in face of parliamentary inquiry into impact of slashing overseas aid.

By Kaamil Ahmed

The UK government has launched a new strategy to advance gender equality around the world on the same day that MPs announced plans to investigate the impact of UK aid cuts on women and girls.

The global strategy, launched by the Foreign, Commonwealth and Development Office (FCDO) on International Women's Day on Wednesday, will, it says, put more focus on gender equality in its work, while also supporting sexual and reproductive health programmes and funding grassroots women's rights groups.

'Advancing gender equality and challenging discrimination is obviously the right thing to do, but it also brings freedom, boosts prosperity and trade, and strengthens security – it is the fundamental building block of all healthy democracies,' said foreign secretary James Cleverly while visiting schools and hospitals in Bo, his mother's home town in Sierra Leone.

'Hard-won gains' in advancing gender equality – by getting more girls into school, reducing child marriage and increasing representation of women at the highest levels of politics – have come under threat, he said, from the climate crisis, conflict and policies by some governments in the world.

But the strategy announcement, the first since the FCDO was created in 2020, came as the International Development Committee (IDC) launched a parliamentary inquiry into the impact of the government's own funding cuts on women and girls in low-income countries.

In 2021, the FCDO confirmed that £4 billion would be cut from the aid budget. Last year, the government was accused of 'betraying' women and girls after it emerged ministers had been warned that aid reductions would have an adverse affect on them.

The IDC said it had received evidence that cuts significantly affected the FCDO's work with women and girls.

'The impact of cutting access to sexual and reproductive health services for women and their families in lower-income countries is huge,' said Sarah Champion, the committee's chair.

'We know that this work can make the ultimate difference. We want to examine how the FCDO is meeting its pledges and will evaluate the impact of cuts to the UK's aid budget in this vital area.'

Last week, the IDC criticised the government for diverting £1 billion in foreign aid to house refugees in the UK in 2021.

Stephanie Siddall, the director of global policy and advocacy at Women for Women International, said the UK aid cuts have had a disproportionate impact on women. 'In conflict and crisis we see increased poverty affecting women and girls, we see girls being unable to access schooling, and we see the drivers and consequences of gender-based violence increasing,' she said.

She said that any new strategy needed funding that would repair the impact of the funding cuts. As part of the strategy, the government said that £200 million will be provided for women's sexual health programmes, while £38 million has been assigned to support women's rights organisations and grassroots movements, which will mostly be distributed through the Equality Fund, which helps fund feminist movements.

Siddall said the amount was a 'drop in the ocean' without a return to the UK spending 0.7% of national income on aid. 'It's all very well having a strategy but the government needs to put its money where its mouth is. It's almost meaningless unless you're going to have an appropriate budget,' she said.

Manali Desai, the head of Cambridge University's sociology department and an expert on gendered violence in India and South Asia, said: 'The FCDO needs to join up its strategy on women and girls to almost every facet of the current challenges facing areas receiving aid. These include poverty, climate change, war, migration and education, among others. Women and girls are affected in very specific ways by these events.'

But Bethan Cobley, the director of advocacy and partnerships at MSI Reproductive Choices, said the new strategy was 'an important first step'. 'Now adequate and sustained resourcing and implementation is vital through FCDO's programme work and global influence,' she said.

8 March 2023

Brainstorm

In small groups, discuss what you know about gender equality. Consider the following:

- What does the term gender equality mean?

- How and where do we learn our perception of male and female gender roles?

- Can you give an example of a situation where you feel you have been discriminated against because of your gender?

Why we need gender equity, not just equality

The theme of this year's International Women's Day campaign is 'embrace equity'. But what is gender equity, and how can we achieve it in the workplace, to the benefit of businesses?

By Emma Crabtree

Equity vs equality

The easiest way of describing the difference between equity and equality is that equality is the end goal and equity is how we get there.

Gender equality is giving all genders equal treatment when it comes to rights, responsibilities and opportunities. Gender equity, meanwhile, is about fairness. To ensure everyone has equal opportunities, we need to consider privilege, bias and other parameters that can limit how people access opportunities.

Inequality has a price

Gender inequality has widespread consequences. Globally, women account for only 38% of human capital wealth. In fact, inequality is costing us all. The World Bank Group estimates that if women had the same lifetime earnings as men, global wealth would increase by $23,620 per person, on average, in the 141 countries studied, for a total of $160 trillion.

This inequality is clearly visible in business; aside from the gender wage gap, women are less likely to progress into leadership positions. According to McKinsey's annual *Women in the Workplace* report, for every 100 men who are promoted from entry-level roles to manager positions, 87 women are promoted, and only 82 women of colour. It has also been shown that women of child-bearing age and women with children are less likely to be considered for jobs.

With gender inequality still prevalent today, organisations have a responsibility to their employees. So, what can we do to change the narrative?

The path to equality is built on equity

Research suggests we're amid a 'Great Breakup.' Women are leaving companies and switching jobs en masse and it's having consequences for organisations who can't keep up.

To promote gender equity, we should understand that a 'one size fits all' approach to employee wellbeing isn't sufficient if we want to optimise talent retention. We should listen to what women want from an employer, most of which fits into three categories: diversity, flexibility and education.

Female leaders tend to want to work for companies that are diverse, inclusive and prioritise employee wellbeing.

Diversity, equality and inclusion (DE&I) initiatives are so important to women but 40% say their DE&I work isn't acknowledged in performance reviews, and spending time and energy on work that isn't recognised makes them feel burned out. Diversity encourages diversity, and this is why it's important to women; when there's representation at the top of the hierarchy, women are more likely to be promoted.

Offering flexibility, whether that's hybrid working or shiftable working hours, entices more women to join an organisation. However, with reports suggesting flexible working patterns also burden women with an increased workload, it's important that this is implemented correctly. Flexible working should still promote choice, giving an employee power to decide what is best suited to their needs.

Lastly, education is key to promoting gender equity. Unconscious bias training makes us all aware of prejudices we might be sharing without realising and encourages us to call out discriminatory behaviour. Furthermore, employee learning and development courses, like ones we have at IQ-EQ, can empower women to put themselves forward for leadership positions, and give them the tools to succeed.

An equal world should be equitable

Promoting gender equity comes with financial incentives too. Companies with a greater proportion of women in senior leadership and C-suite roles earn a 47% higher rate of return on equity compared with companies who had no women executives.

In the finance sphere, equity represents the value that would be returned to shareholders if all assets were liquidated and the debts were paid off. It presents an opportunity for reward, sometimes an investment – and the same mindset can be applied when discussing the implications of gender equity.

Equity is the investment, equality is the reward, and we all make a profit.

8 March 2023

Women and men at work

An extract from: *Inequality: The IFS Deaton Review*

By Alison Andrew, Institute for Fiscal Studies, Oriana Bandiera, London School of Economics, Monica Costa Dias, Institute for Fiscal Studies and Camille Landais, London School of Economics

This chapter is concerned with the differences between men and women in all activities that can be labelled as 'work' – that is, the time and energy that people devote to producing things of value. Work thus encompasses the production of market goods and service as well as the time spent doing household chores, childcare or care of the elderly.

- The average working-age woman in the UK earned 40% less than her male counterpart in 2019. That gap is about 13 percentage points, or 25%, lower than it was 25 years ago.

- The vast majority of the modest convergence in earnings of the past 25 years can be explained by the closing of the gender gap in education levels. Of the 13 percentage point drop in the gender pay gap, 10 percentage points (or over three-quarters) would have been expected from the rapid catch-up of educational attainment of women, who are now 5% more likely to have graduated from university than men. This suggests that the additional contribution to closing the gender earnings gap from other changes in policy, the economy and society over the past quarter-century has been muted.

- Inequalities in all three components of labour market earnings – employment, working hours and hourly wages – remained large. In 2019, working women still earned 19% less per hour than men. This gap was 5 percentage points smaller than the gap in the mid 1990s, though again women's relative advances in education can account for the majority of the gain.

- Gaps in all three components are linked. The fact that women have more career breaks and years working part-time contributes to them having lower hourly earnings further down the line.

- In a big break from the past, the hourly wage gap between men and women is now bigger for those with degrees or A-level-equivalent qualifications than for those with lower education. It used to be that gender differences in hourly wages were especially large among less-well-educated workers. The introduction of, and increases to, the UK's minimum wage have been an important factor in helping low-paid women. More highly educated women have not made comparable progress.

- Gender gaps in hourly wage rates are especially large at the top, with women failing to reach the same levels of high pay as men. In 2019, women at the top (90th percentile) earned per hour only 77% of what their male counterparts did, while that figure was about 90% for women at the bottom (10th percentile) compared with men at the same level.

- Gender differences in time spent doing paid work are not completely balanced out by the differences in time doing unpaid domestic work. In the UK, working-age women on average do 1.5 fewer hours of paid work and 1.8 more hours of unpaid work per day than men.

- Gender gaps in pay, paid work and unpaid work have substantial consequences for inequalities in material living standards. Women in single-adult families, especially single mothers, are especially vulnerable to poverty. Women in opposite-gender couple families have been found to consume less than their male partners.

- Inequalities in earnings and its three components increase vastly after parenthood. The opening of gaps around childbirth suggests that unpaid care work is central in shaping inequalities in the labour market.

- The gendered roles that mothers and fathers take on appear to be largely unrelated to their relative earnings potential. Even mothers who earn more than their male partners before childbirth are more likely than their partners to reduce hours of work in the years after childbirth.

- The existing policy environment (including parental leave, childcare, and the tax and benefit system) often sustains and incentivises a traditionally gendered division of labour, even when policies are ostensibly gender-neutral. For instance, welfare subsidies that are taxed away with family income will disincentivise the work of a second earner, who is usually the woman. At the same time, policies designed to incentivise a more equal division of labour often have quite muted effects.

- At the level of the whole economy and society, these heavily gendered patterns of paid and unpaid work strongly suggest that the talents of women and men are not being used in the most productive way possible. This means that, overall, the economy produces less

(both market goods and services and unpaid care) than would be possible if the talents of women and men were allocated more efficiently.

- Norms, preferences and beliefs appear central to the choices of families. Two-fifths of both men and women in the UK agree that 'a woman should stay at home when she has children under school age'. Internationally, there is huge variation in the proportion of the population who hold traditional gender attitudes. The extent of agreement with such statements is strongly positively correlated with gender gaps in labour market outcomes.

- However, these constructs are not immutable. An accumulation of policies consistently supporting a more equal sharing of responsibilities between parents (or large policy reforms challenging gender roles) may help build up a change in attitudes that leads to permanent change in norms. Given the huge economic costs associated with the status quo, even expensive policies could potentially pay for themselves if they successfully ensure that the talents of both women and men are put to their most productive uses, whether in the labour market or at home.

6 December 2021

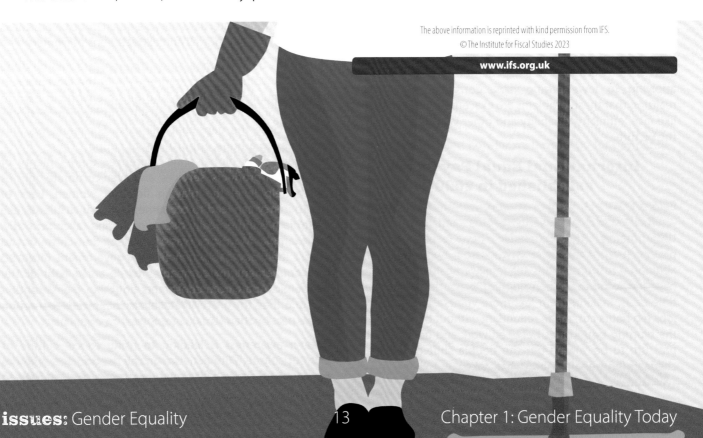

The importance of good childcare services for gender equality

Professor Ingela Naumann at Fribourg University discusses the impacts of the COVID-19 pandemic on childcare arrangements and family wellbeing, and how it highlighted gendered care norms.

Ingela Naumann, Fribourg University

The COVID-pandemic put a spotlight on a central conundrum of modern society: you cannot do your job while simultaneously looking after your child. Whatever you do, in the long run one or the other will suffer: You can park your child in front of the TV so you can do that online meeting (bad educational value!), or you pretend to be present in that meeting while, actually, you are stacking blocks with your child (and you might miss that important part in the meeting for your input!). Yet, during COVID-lockdowns when childcare services and schools were closed and employment moved online for many, scores of parents tried to do exactly that: juggle employment and childcare in their homes, all at once. How did they fare?

How did the COVID-19 pandemic affect the childcare arrangements and wellbeing of families?

In a UK-based research project that analysed representative data from several longitudinal surveys and conducted interviews with a large number of parents on their experiences during the COVID-pandemic, we found that stress levels and exhaustion amongst parents rose significantly as a consequence of their continuous 'multi-tasking'. Parents were more at risk of mental health problems during the pandemic than non- parents, and the worst affected were mothers.

There is a clear gendered picture to the pandemic: it was women who shouldered the extra demands of increased childcare responsibilities, homeschooling and more hours of domestic work, many juggling these with paid employment. What's more, many women experienced a 'double whammy' with increased employment demands, for example as nurses and care workers. It was also mostly women who cut back on their working hours or quit their jobs where it was not possible to combine the multiple pressures, for example in large families with several children or in one-parent families. Notably, we also found that where mothers suffered a sharp decline in their mental health also their children were at risk of poorer mental wellbeing.

Women in the UK are not alone in their experiences, research from around the world corroborates these findings. The gendered costs of the COVID- pandemic were experienced on a global scale.

Why good childcare services are so important for society

While the COVID-pandemic and the measures needed to contain the virus such as social distancing were new experiences for us all, the challenges involved in juggling work and care responsibilities are not, of course. The COVID-pandemic only exacerbated what is for many parents, particularly mothers, an everyday struggle – and thus

Figure 1: Descriptive statistics on proportion of young adults (30-31) 'feeling more stressed' in the pandemic compared to before.

Source: Longitudinal Cohort Studies (Covid-19) survey, 'Next steps' cohort, gathered in May 2020

Figure 2: How childcare was shared between men and women during the pandemic

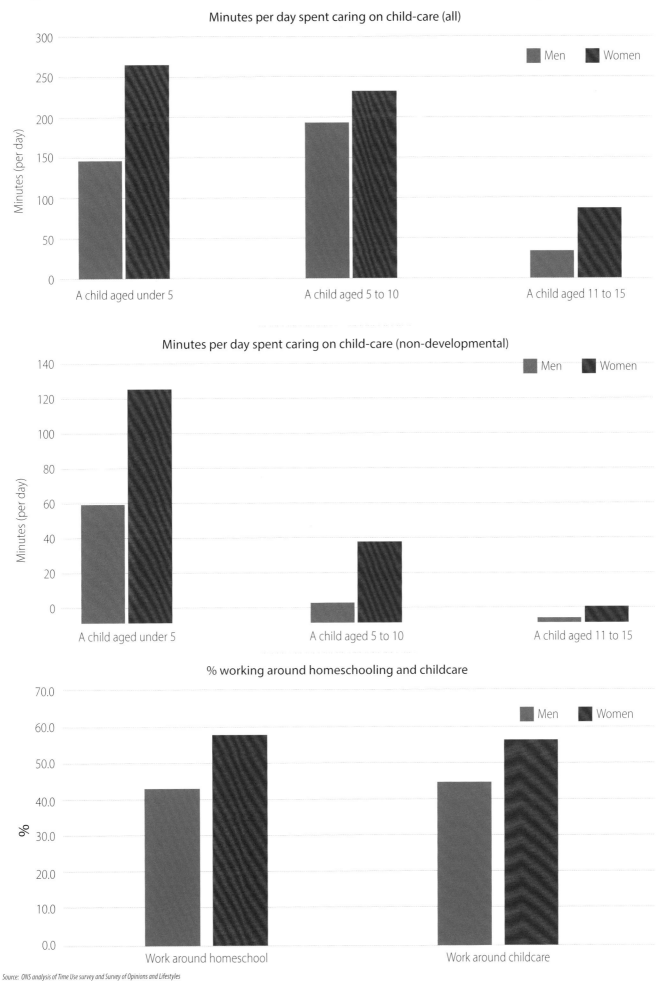

Minutes per day spent caring on child-care (all)

Minutes per day spent caring on child-care (non-developmental)

% working around homeschooling and childcare

Source: ONS analysis of Time Use survey and Survey of Opinions and Lifestyles

reminded us of the importance of good, affordable, and accessible childcare services.

Good childcare services can support parents in engaging in gainful employment and thus bolster families against economic insecurity; they can mitigate that 'double shift' that parents, particularly mothers, cope with, thus supporting better health outcomes for parents as well as for their children. And finally, good quality childcare services support early childhood development and can thus help address the educational attainment gaps often experienced by children from disadvantaged backgrounds. That is why 'childcare' these days has been replaced by the term 'early childhood education and care' (ECEC) – to emphasize this double function with respect to parental employment and early education.

Women are caught between employment ideals and gendered care norms

As mature welfare states have begun to model reforms to their social security systems around the guiding principle of the 'adult worker model' which links social benefits closer to contributions made via gainful employment, well-developed universal ECEC provision becomes even more central. For those members of society who cannot fulfil the 'adult worker norm' due to care responsibilities are disadvantaged and at risk of financial insecurity such as old age poverty. This affects particularly women due to providing the bulk of unpaid care in society.

Only few countries have universal ECEC provision fit to fully support parental employment

Across the OECD, countries have begun to recognize the importance of ECEC to society and expanded its provision over the last decades. However, to date, only a small group of countries can be said to have developed ECEC systems that are fit to fully support parental employment – led by

the Nordic countries that acknowledged the systemic role of ECEC early on, in the 1970s. Meanwhile, in most OECD countries, there still exist considerable gaps in ECEC provision, particularly for children under the age of three and with respect to affordable full-time services (OECD 2020).

To take developments in the UK again as an example: while an entitlement to 30 hours of ECEC has been introduced for children aged 3 and 4 (in England, Wales and Scotland), no such entitlement exists for Under-3s. Parents who need childcare services for younger children or need more than 30 hours for 3-4 year-olds to match full-time or longer part-time working hours have to rely mainly on private and expensive childcare services, with low public subsidies. The recent Coram Childcare Survey found that a full-time nursery place for a 2-year-old costs on average as much as 50.2% of average full-time pay in the London area (and 35.5% in Scotland). This is unaffordable for many families, and particularly mothers are being 'priced out of employment' having to give up their job or reduce working hours.*

Why childcare is key to gender equality

In light of the persistence of gendered care norms in most societies that became so apparent during the COVID-pandemic, a lack of affordable and accessible childcare services remains a serious obstacle to gender equality, and negatively affects women, children and society at large. Further efforts to expand childcare provision and increase public funding are needed in many OECD countries.

* In acknowledgement of this situation, the UK Government recently announced it is set to expand the 30 hours childcare entitlement to children aged 2 and 1.

24 April 2023

New Zealand makes history with gender parity in cabinet

'Clearly, it is nice to have a cabinet that reflects the New Zealand population.'

By Alisha Rahaman Sarkar

New Zealand's cabinet has achieved gender equality for the first time in the country's history, less than a week after its third female leader Jacinda Ardern bade an emotional farewell to politics.

Parity was achieved on Tuesday with 10 women and 10 male members in cabinet after prime minister Chris Hipkins announced a reshuffle, promoting MP Willow-Jean Prime as conservation minister.

'For the first time in New Zealand's history, half of the people sitting around the cabinet table will be women,' the prime minister said.

'Clearly, it is nice to have a cabinet that reflects the New Zealand population,' Mr Hipkins said, according to The New Zealand Herald.

'And in fact, overall, there are more women in the executive than there are men if you count the ministers outside of the cabinet as well.'

The MP for Northland, Ms Prime will also hold the portfolios of minister of youth and associate minister for health and for arts and culture.

Mr Hipkins said although he was pleased to have achieved gender parity, it wasn't a decisive factor in the reshuffle.

He said Ms Prime was chosen because of her 'skills as a person and the portfolios she currently holds'.

'I'm confident that you'll be a very active contributor around the cabinet table,' he said in comments addressed to Ms Prime. 'I feel fortunate in the sense that there are a lot of choices there.'

The Pacific nation elected its most diverse and inclusive parliament ever under Ms Ardern, who resigned as prime minister in January after more than five years in office, saying she no longer felt she had 'enough in the tank' to lead.

Ms Ardern's final cabinet included five Māori MPs, eight women and members of the LGBT+ community.

Her and Mr Hipkins' Labour Party won the last election by a landslide in 2020, with 58 women across all parties in the 120-member parliament. A number of resignations later boosted that total to 61, when the country made history with female MPs outnumbering their male counterparts for the first time.

Soraya Peke-Mason tipped women into the majority in October last year when she was sworn into parliament.

Mr Hipkins, who entered office in January, has promoted three women to his cabinet, with Wellington-based MPs Ginny Andersen and Barbara Edmonds added as part of the prime minister's first reshuffle.

11 April 2023

Research

In the current UK government, how many female MPs have a position in the Cabinet Office? How does that compare to other countries around the world?

International Women's Day: global opinion remains committed to gender equality, but half now believe it is coming at the expense of men

Ipsos unveils a new global study carried out in 32 countries in collaboration with the Global Institute for Women's Leadership at King's College London for International Women's Day 2023.

Jessica Bruce, Public Affairs and Olivia Ryan, Public Affairs

Key takeaways

- 7 in 10 (68%) agree there is currently inequality between men and women in terms of social, political, and/or economic rights in their country, down slightly from 2017.

- However, 1 in 2 (54%) say that when it comes to giving women equal rights with men, things have gone far enough in their country – gradually increasing since 2019.

- There are concerns about the impact of equality on men, with half (54%) agreeing men are being expected to do too much to support equality (also up from 2019), and half (48%) agreeing that things have gone so far in promoting women's equality that men are being discriminated against.

- Even so, 3 in 5 (62%) agree there are actions they can take to help promote equality, with a similar share (56%) reporting they have taken at least one action in the past year. But there is also evidence of barriers, with over 1 in 3 (37%) feeling scared to speak out for women's rights

because of what might happen to them – higher than in 2017.

Most agree that there is inequality between men and women - but differ on whether men benefit from gender equality

Looking at respondents across all generations globally, the majority agree that inequality between men and women persists, and that improvements will require efforts from both men and women. A global country average of 68% agree there is currently inequality between men and women in terms of social, political, and/or economic rights in their country (looking at the trend since 2017 across a sub-sample of 22 countries, the proportion who believe inequality exists has fallen by 5 points since then). There is a similar level of agreement that women won't achieve equality in their country unless men take action to support women's rights (64% global country average), and that there are actions people can personally take to help promote equality between men and women (62%).

Gender inequality across the world

To what extent do you agree with the following statement: 'I believe there is currently an inequality between women and men in terms of social, political and/or economic rights in my country'.

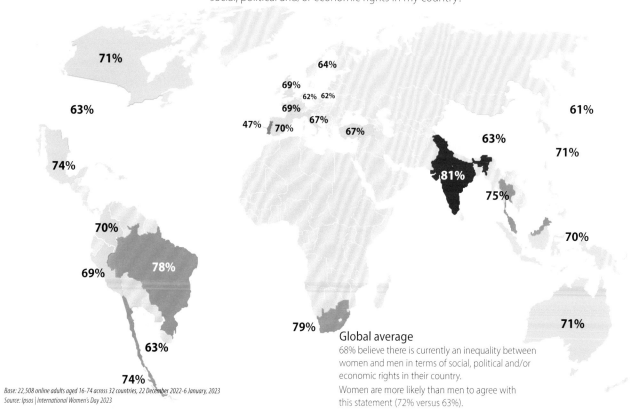

Global average
68% believe there is currently an inequality between women and men in terms of social, political and/or economic rights in their country.
Women are more likely than men to agree with this statement (72% versus 63%).

Base: 22,508 online adults aged 16-74 across 32 countries, 22 December 2022-6 January, 2023
Source: Ipsos | International Women's Day 2023

Global views on gender equality

Below is a list of statements. For each indicate whether you strongly disagree, somewhat disagree, somewhat agree, or strongly agree.

▨ Agree somewhat/strongly	▨ Don't know	▨ Disagree somewhat/strongly

Women won't achieve equality in... unless men take actions to support women's rights too

64%	10%	26%

Equality between men and women will be achieved in my lifetime

55%	14%	31%

When it comes to giving women equal rights with men, things have gone far enough in my country

54%	8%	38%

Base: 22,508 online adults aged 16-74 across 32 countries, 22 December 2022-6 January, 2023

Source: Ipsos Global Advisor | International Women's Day 2023

Just over half (55%) believe equality between men and women will be achieved in their lifetime – across the 25 countries who took part in 2018 and 2023, optimism that equality will be achieved is 5 points higher than before the Covid pandemic. In line with this, people around the world tend to believe young people will have a better life than their parents' generation – although a larger proportion feel optimistic about the future of young women (51% global country average) than for young men (42%).

When asked whether gender equality mainly benefits women, mainly benefits men, or is good for both men and women, half (53%) say it is good for both genders, with a further 1 in 5 (18%) saying it mainly benefits women. Men are more likely than women to agree that gender equality mainly benefits women (22% of men compared to 13% of women). Only 8% say that gender equality mainly benefits men.

Despite this, a majority (54% global country average) also agree that when it comes to giving women equal rights with men, things have gone far enough in their country – an identical proportion (54%) say that men are expected to

do too much to support equality. Indeed, 48% agree that we have gone so far in promoting women's equality that we're discriminating against men. And there are signs that these views are held more widely now than before the Covid pandemic. On average across 25 countries, the proportion of people who think men are being expected to do too much to support equality has risen by 9 points from 43% to 52% between 2019 and 2023. At the same time, there has been a 7-point rise in the belief that things have gone far enough when it comes to giving women equal rights, from 42% to 49%.

Day-to-day incidents of sexism persist, but most say they're able to take action - despite increasing belief that there's risk in doing so

4 in 10 (43% global country average) report having witnessed at least one of several forms of gender discrimination in the past year, with the most common being hearing a friend or family member make a sexist comment (27%), followed by seeing examples of gender

Taking action: what people do?

In the past year, have you done any of the following things, or not?

Talked about gender equality with your family or friends

32%

Spoke up when a friend or family member made a sexist comment

21%

Talked about gender equality at work

21%

Signing an online or paper petition for gender equality

12%

Talked to employers/senior managers at work about examples of gender discrimination at work

12%

Confronted someone who was sexually harassing a woman

12%

Participated in a protest for gender equality in person

8%

Told someone you're a feminist

7%

None of the above

37%

Any of the above

56%

Base: 22,508 online adults aged 16-74 across 32 countries, 22 December 2022-6 January, 2023

Source: Ipsos Global Advisor | International Women's Day 2023

discrimination at work (20%), and seeing someone sexually harass a woman (14%).

3 in 5 (59%) say they've taken at least one action to promote gender equality in the past year. The most common actions taken include talking about gender equality with family or friends (32%), speaking up when a friend or family member made a sexist comment (21%), and talking about gender equality at work (21%). Over 1 in 3 (37%) said they have taken no action in the past year.

However, there is also evidence of the barriers that are preventing people from taking action to support gender inequality. Over 1 in 3 (global country average of 37%) say they are scared to speak out and advocate the equal rights of women because of what might happen to them. This too has increased over the last 6 years: between 2017 and 2023, the average proportion across 22 countries feeling scared to speak out has risen from 24% to 33%.

When asked directly, respondents also named other barriers: feeling that there's nothing people can do that will really make a difference (13%), not knowing how to talk about gender equality/what next steps should be taken (11%), feeling that it's irrelevant/unimportant (10%), and feeling concerned about being physically abused or threatened (10%). More positively, the least commonly selected responses were that it's only a women's issue (asked of men only; 6%), that people don't think gender equality exists (6%), and that they don't want to promote it (5%).

Younger generations are more optimistic about the future than older age groups, but they are also more cautious about the risk of speaking out and are more concerned that gender equality negatively impacts men

On average across all 32 countries surveyed, Gen Z (45%) and Millennials (44%) are more likely to identify as feminists, compared to 37% of Gen X and 36% of Baby Boomers. Furthermore, 2 in 3 Gen Z (65%) and Millennials (65%) agree there are actions they can take to promote equality between men and women, as do 61% of Gen X, but falling to 52% of Baby Boomers. Similarly, younger generations are more likely to agree that gender equality will be achieved in their lifetime (60% of Gen Z and 61% of Millennials, vs 53% of Gen X and 44% of Baby Boomers). Gen Z are also the most likely to have taken at least one of the listed actions in support of gender equality in the past year (68%), and this falls steadily with each generation, with Baby Boomers the least likely to have taken action (41%).

This optimism comes despite a larger share of Gen Z (48%) and Millennials (43%) saying they're scared to speak out for women's equal rights because of what might happen to them, a fear shared by 1 in 3 Gen Xers (32%) and only 1 in 4 Baby Boomers (23%). The younger generations are also more likely to say they've seen at least one form of discrimination

Taking action: what barriers do people face?

There are many different reasons why people may not talk about gender equality or take actions about it.
What, if anything, has stopped you from taking action towards gender equality in the past year?

There's nothing I can do that will really make a difference

13%

I don't know how to talk about gender/equality what steps I should take

11%

It's not relevant/important to me

10%

I am worried I might be physically abused or threatened because of it

10%

I don't have time

9%

I am worried about what others will think of me

8%

I am worried it will damage my own career/situation

8%

I find it embarrassing

7%

Gender inequality doesn't exist

6%

I don't want to promote gender equality

5%

It's only a woman's issue (asked to men only)

6%

There is nothing stopping me, I take action regularly

17%

I have never been in a situation where I've seen an example of gender inequality

14%

Base: 22,508 online adults aged 16-74 across 32 countries, 22 December 2022-6 January, 2023

Source: Ipsos Global Advisor | International Women's Day 2023

mentioned in the survey (58% Gen Z and 49% Millennials compared with 36% Gen X and 26% of Baby Boomers).

At the same time, about half of Gen Z (52%) and Millennials (53%) agree that things have gone so far in promoting women's equality that men are being discriminated against, falling to 46% of Gen X and 40% of Baby Boomers. Younger generations are also the most likely to agree that a man who stays home to look after his children is less of a man, with 30% each of Gen Z and Millennials agreeing with this statement compared to 22% of Gen X and just 14% of Baby Boomers.

About this study

These are the results of a 32-country survey conducted by Ipsos on its Global Advisor online platform. Ipsos interviewed a total of 22,508 adults aged 18-74 in the United States, Canada, Malaysia, South Africa, and Turkey, 20-74 in Thailand, 21-74 in Indonesia and Singapore and 16-74 in 24 other markets between Friday, December 22, 2022 and Friday, January 6, 2023.

8 March 2023

www.ipsos.com

Britons increasingly scared to speak out on women's rights, data shows

The share of the public who feel this way has doubled in five years.

People in Britain are increasingly afraid of promoting women's rights for fear of reprisals, a major 32-country survey conducted for International Women's Day has found.

The share of the British public who say they are scared to speak out and advocate for the equal rights of women because of what might happen to them has doubled since 2017, rising from 14% to 29%. The majority, though, continue to say this does not apply to them (71%).

International Women's Day 2023 survey

This growing sense of fear is in line with the direction of travel elsewhere in the world: across all the countries included in the study, an average of 37% now say they are afraid to speak out – and looking across 22 nations for which

trends are available, the proportion who say this applies to them has risen from 24% to 33% since 2017.

The research, by Ipsos UK and the Global Institute for Women's Leadership at King's College London, finds that younger generations in Britain tend to be most fearful, with Gen Z (38%) around twice as likely as Baby Boomers (19%) to feel this way.

Across a range of other issues, the study reveals some shifts in public opinion that could suggest Britons are becoming more hostile to the idea of gender equality, as well as other shifts that are potentially more positive.

Yet the findings also highlight that future progress is not guaranteed, with younger generations in fact holding less supportive views on some aspects of gender equality, even

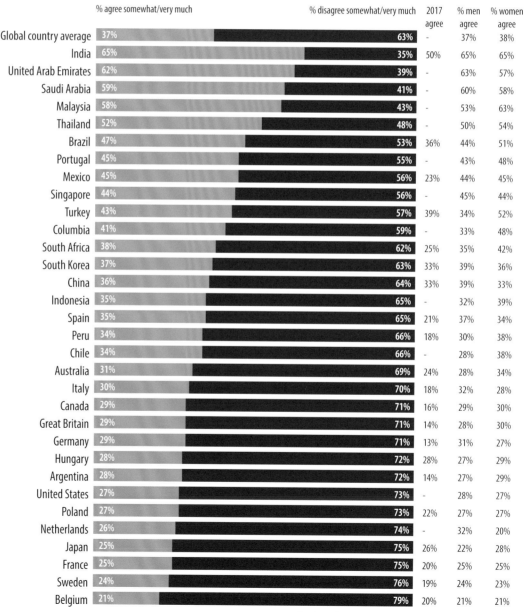

Q: To what extent do you agree or disagree with the following statement?

I am scared to speak out and advocate the rights of women because of what might happen to me

Almost two in five people (37%) are scared to speak out and advocate the equal rights of women because of what might happen to them, with similar proportions of men and women agreeing with this statement globally.

	% agree somewhat/very much	% disagree somewhat/very much	2017 agree	% men agree	% women agree
Global country average	37%	63%	-	37%	38%
India	65%	35%	50%	65%	65%
United Arab Emirates	62%	39%	-	63%	57%
Saudi Arabia	59%	41%	-	60%	58%
Malaysia	58%	43%	-	53%	63%
Thailand	52%	48%	-	50%	54%
Brazil	47%	53%	36%	44%	51%
Portugal	45%	55%	-	43%	48%
Mexico	45%	56%	23%	44%	45%
Singapore	44%	56%	-	45%	44%
Turkey	43%	57%	39%	34%	52%
Columbia	41%	59%	-	33%	48%
South Africa	38%	62%	25%	35%	42%
South Korea	37%	63%	33%	39%	36%
China	36%	64%	33%	39%	33%
Indonesia	35%	65%	-	32%	39%
Spain	35%	65%	21%	37%	34%
Peru	34%	66%	18%	30%	38%
Chile	34%	66%	-	28%	38%
Australia	31%	69%	24%	28%	34%
Italy	30%	70%	18%	32%	28%
Canada	29%	71%	16%	29%	30%
Great Britain	29%	71%	14%	28%	30%
Germany	29%	71%	13%	31%	27%
Hungary	28%	72%	28%	27%	29%
Argentina	28%	72%	14%	27%	29%
United States	27%	73%	-	28%	27%
Poland	27%	73%	22%	27%	27%
Netherlands	26%	74%	-	32%	20%
Japan	25%	75%	26%	22%	28%
France	25%	75%	20%	25%	25%
Sweden	24%	76%	19%	24%	23%
Belgium	21%	79%	20%	21%	21%

Base: 22,508 online adults aged 16-17 across 32 countries, 22 December 2022 - 6 January 2023

Source: Ipsos - International Women's Day 2023

if they are still most likely to describe themselves as feminist and to say they've taken various actions to promote equality in the past year.

Some trends suggest a growing resistance to gender equality in Britain

- 38% now agree that when it comes to giving women equal rights with men, things have gone far enough – up from 25% in 2018.

- 38% also feel that men are being expected to do too much to support equality, an increase on the 29% who felt this way in 2019.

- The share of the British public who say that a man who stays home to look after his children is less of a man has risen slightly, from 13% in 2019 to 19% today, with men (23%) more likely than women (14%) to feel this way.

And a large minority of the British public – two in five (43%) people – say we have gone so far in promoting women's equality that we are discriminating against men. A majority of men (53%) agree with this view, as well as a third of women (33%).

But other trends are heading in a more positive direction

- 47% of Britons now think equality between men and women will be achieved within their lifetime, compared with 40% in 2018.

- A majority of 51% agree there are actions they can take to help promote equality between men and women – a slight rise from 46% five years ago.

And Britain is still among the most supportive of gender equality internationally

Of 32 countries, only three – Poland (26%), Japan (21%) and Portugal (17%) – are less likely than Britain (38%) to feel giving women equality with men has gone far enough.

And the share of the British public (38%) who think men are being expected to do too much to support equality is on a par with the share in the US (36%), which is least likely to agree with this view.

Britons are also comparatively unlikely to say they've heard a friend or family member make a sexist comment about a woman in the past year. One in five (18%) report hearing such a comment, with only people in South Korea (14%) and Japan (6%) less likely to report the same.

Younger generations do not always have the most progressive views on gender equality

It is often assumed that younger generations will inevitably be most supportive of efforts to advance gender equality – but this is not always the case. Looking at the global country average across the 32 nations included in the survey reveals the following:

- Gen Z (30%) and Millennials (30%) are twice as likely as Baby Boomers (14%) to say that a man who stays home to look after his children is less of a man, with a similar pattern seen in Britain.

- Majorities of Gen Z (52%) and Millennials (53%) say we have gone so far in promoting women's equality that we are discriminating against men – greater than the share of Baby Boomers (40%) and Gen X (46%) who say the same.

- And Baby Boomers – the oldest cohort surveyed – are in fact least likely to agree that when it comes to giving women equal rights with men, things have gone far enough in their country (44%, versus 54% of Gen Z) and to agree that men are being expected to do too much to support equality (47%, versus 55% of Gen Z). In Britain, we see the latter but not the former.

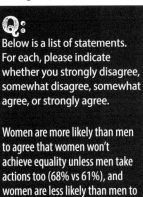

Q: Below is a list of statements. For each, please indicate whether you strongly disagree, somewhat disagree, somewhat agree, or strongly agree.

Women are more likely than men to agree that women won't achieve equality unless men take actions too (68% vs 61%), and women are less likely than men to believe that equality will be achieved in their lifetime (52% vs 58%).

Men are more likely to believe that when it comes to giving women equal rights with men, things have gone far enough in their country (58% vs 49%). More than half of all men (55%) believe that we have gone so far in promoting women's equality that we are discriminating against men (vs 41% of women).

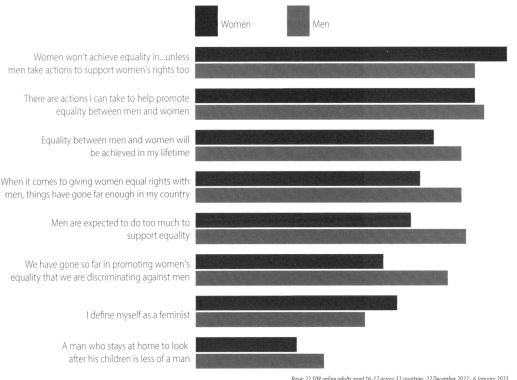

Base: 22,508 online adults aged 16-17 across 32 countries, 22 December 2022 - 6 January 2023
Source: Ipsos - International Women's Day 2023

Q: Below is a list of statements. For each, please indicate whether you strongly disagree, somewhat disagree. somewhat agree, or strongly agree.

Younger generations tend to be more optimistic than older generations that equality between men and women will be achieved in their lifetime and are more likely to define themselves as a feminist. They are however, also more likely then older generations to think thta we have gone so far in promoting women's equality that we are discriminating against men.

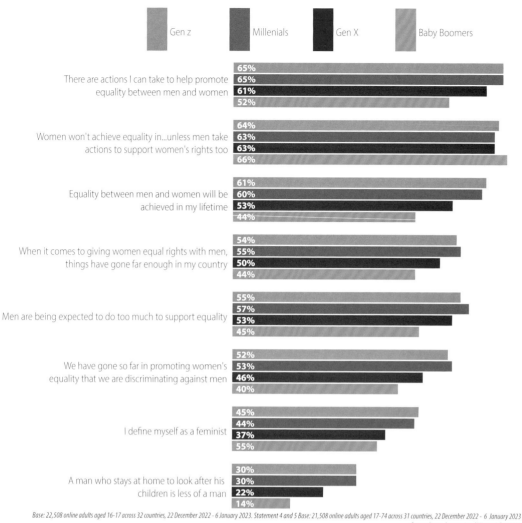

Base: 22,508 online adults aged 16-17 across 32 countries, 22 December 2022 - 6 January 2023. Statement 4 and 5 Base: 21,508 online adults aged 17-74 across 31 countries, 22 December 2022 - 6 January 2023

Source: Ipsos - International Women's Day 2023

Yet younger generations are more open about other aspects of gender equality, highlighting there is no uniform view among cohorts. For example, Gen Z (45%) and Millennials (44%) are more likely than Gen X (37%) and Baby Boomers (35%) to say they define themselves as a feminist. A similar divide is found in Britain.

And Gen Z stand out as most likely to say that in the past year they have spoken up when a friend or family member made a sexist comment (27%, versus 16% of Baby Boomers), a pattern also seen in Britain.

Gen Z are also most likely to say they've confronted someone who was sexually harassing a woman (17%, versus 7% of Baby Boomers) – though they are also more likely to have been in these situations in the first place.

Overall, across the 32 countries surveyed, 68% of Gen Z say they have taken at least one action to promote gender equality in the past year, compared with 41% of Baby Boomers.

Kelly Beaver MBE, chief executive of Ipsos, UK and Ireland, said:

'Our ongoing research into gender equality shows that we have made significant progress with nearly half of people now agreeing equality will be achieved within their lifetime. However, there are signs that the public are starting to push back on this progress to date, which is potentially worrying, but it may also be a sign that real change is happening in society and change can often make people uncomfortable and

resistant. Over the coming years we will continue to measure this shift and I hope that we will see this discomfort shift to acceptance, acceptance that achieving gender equality is an essential evolution for British society.'

Julia Gillard, chair of the Global Institute for Women's Leadership at King's College London, said:

'Despite the progress we've made in recent decades, high-profile examples of misogyny are still rife, particularly online, and there are worrying signs from this research that such views are not only gaining ground among the public, but also deterring people from advocating for women's rights. No one should be afraid to promote equality, and we need to do much better in supporting people to call out injustice wherever they see it.

'But we should also emphasise the positives where we find them, including that people are increasingly likely to identify as a feminist and to recognise there are things they can do to improve gender equality. Yet we mustn't be complacent. That it's younger generations who are most likely to say a man who stays home to look after his children is less of a man is a disturbing reminder there is still much more to do, and that future progress is not guaranteed.'

8 March 2023

The Lionesses roar: what next for equality in football?

Carrie Dunn, author of a history of women's football, speaks to experts about gender equality in the sport – and finds that the issues within the game are found across society.

Where there's success, there's talk of money. England's Lionesses hadn't even packed away their gold medals after winning UEFA Women's EURO 2022 before the murmurs began about their salaries. After all, the men's senior team haven't won anything since 1966 and they get paid millions. Why shouldn't the women get the same?

Since 2020, England's international teams – male and female – have received a match fee from the Football Association (FA) of around £2,000. All the men donate that to charity as do some of the women.

The bonuses on offer at major tournaments, however, are somewhat different. If the women had won the World Cup in 2019, they would have got £50,000 each. Had the men won their tournament in Russia the year before, they were in line to get £217,000 each.

That's because the FIFA prize funds – the pot put together by the governing body of world football – are different, and depend hugely on the advertising and broadcast deals each tournament has brought in.

'The resources that you put into that team will be vastly different because how much money the country stands to win is vastly different,' says Dr Alex Culvin, a former footballer who now works in player relations for Fifpro, the international players' union.

'It's a very simplified, straightforward way of quantifying [the pay] differences between men and women. But actually they have very different starting points.'

The Lionesses are earning decent money. They will have a central contract with the FA for their international appearances, worth about £30,000 depending on their age and their experience.

That is on top of the salary they receive from their clubs. The top tier in England, the Women's Super League, is one of the best-paid in the world, and boasts its own broadcasting deal as well as sponsorship from Barclays. Chelsea's Australian international Sam Kerr is thought to be on a significant salary, although there are no definite figures. It has been estimated by some to be more than £350,000 a year.

Arsenal's Vivianne Miedema signed a new contract with her club in March, and although she didn't give any figures, she revealed: 'There have been two clubs where I could have made more money, but I think I can say that I will be the highest-paid [women's] footballer in England. So I certainly can't complain.'

But the average professional footballer in the Women's Super League will earn much less than the biggest names in the women's game. When the league first started in 2011, many players worked in second jobs to supplement their income for what was essentially a semi-professional league. Now a basic salary would start at around £20,000.

And of course that is also a striking contrast to the average male Premier League player, who Statista estimates earns around £2.5 million per year, although this salary can drop significantly if a team is relegated or a player moves to a club in a lower league.

Men do tend to play more matches, with more teams in the Premier League than in the Women's Super League. That does not completely explain, says Dr Culvin, the disparity in wages.

'It reduces athletes and what they do to a monetary basis and the reason that is problematic is because it masks a lot of inequalities that exist as well as unequal pay,' Dr Culvin told Byline Times.

'There is no magic number of games you should play per season. The men are overworked, maybe the women are underworked... actually, we've got to ask the question whether playing more games, and again being able to quantify women's value in very direct binary terms, is the way to do it.'

Change is happening

One big leap forward came recently, with maternity rights included in women's contracts.

It might seem obvious to ensure that women players have the right to take time off should they choose to have a baby. But the entire set-up of professional women's football in England is still somewhat in flux.

This is the first generation of full-time professional female footballers who have progressed through talent pathways to reach the top. That means that female professional footballers are expected to fulfil different responsibilities beyond playing matches.

'Think about the emotional labour,' says Dr Culvin. 'You don't get men saying 'our game is this weekend. Please come and watch us'. [Women] are expected to do it. It's not in the contract and they're not remunerated for it, and yet they are expected to carry the game on their shoulders, which men are not expected to do.'

Indeed, England captain Leah Williamson did just that in a television interview immediately after winning the European title, asking viewers to continue their support for the women's game throughout the domestic season. It's hard to imagine any male footballer winning any trophy – regardless of profile or level – and asking the same.

One club which pays their semi-professional male and female players equally are Lewes FC. Its women's team plays in the Championship, the second tier of competition. Lewes FC is committed to equality throughout the club that goes beyond finances and into structures.

'People always want to jump to the money straightaway,' club CEO Maggie Murphy told Byline Times. 'And what I try to say is that it's actually really about equal decision-making, and everything else falls in with trying to build an ethical, community-oriented, transparent, well governed football club.

'When you try to do that, then equality follows suit, and that's why we split our pay equally, because we think it's the right thing to do for our community and for the world.'

It is easy and understandable to be interested in players' salaries and the disparity between men's and women's wages. But the experiences of Lewes FC, and the burden identified by Dr Alex Culvin, suggest that it is not necessarily helpful. When it comes to equality in football, there are bigger questions to be addressed that reach out beyond the pitch.

Expecting women to perform emotional labour, or put up with limited financial support or recognition, is hardly unusual. These issues are not just football's, but found across society.

3 August 2022

Obstacles to Equality

When employers reward 'ideal' workers, gender equality suffers

An article from The Conversation.

By Shireen Kanji, Professor of Work and Organisation, Brunel University London

U K deputy prime minister Dominic Raab recently resigned following the publication of a report into workplace complaints about his conduct, including bullying allegations. But this element of his behaviour wasn't the only concerning workplace problem highlighted by the report.

It also detailed how, seemingly unencumbered by responsibilities outside work, his working hours ran from 7:30am until 10pm, Monday to Thursday, while Fridays were spent on constituency business, usually followed by extensive work on weekends.

When organisations or leaders support such working practices – either by working long hours themselves or rewarding those that do – it can deepen inequality in the workplace. Setting an expectation that it's OK (or even necessary) to work beyond your contracted hours disadvantages those that need more flexibility, such as carers, who are typically women.

Unfortunately, long hours are essentially a requirement for promotion in many managerial and professional jobs. Such working practices accord with the very values that led to the emergence of modern capitalism and the creation of the concept of the 'ideal worker', as argued by sociologist Max Weber. It's hardly surprising, then, that many organisations value and require long hours, even if they are inefficient.

But long working hours undermine health, raising the risks of cardiovascular disease, chronic fatigue, stress, depression, sleep quality, self-perceived health, use of alcohol and cigarettes, and a host of other conditions and problems. Inefficiently long hours could also contribute to low productivity, as well as promoting gender inequality at work and in the home.

Work flexibility versus career progression

Feminist scholars have also long pointed to the adverse effects of long hours on women in particular. Research shows this is a key source of the gender wage gap disadvantage. The UK's Equal Pay Act made a substantial difference in narrowing the gender pay gap, but long working hours still stand in the way of this progress – particularly for those who have caring responsibilities, such as mothers. It is partly because of care that the gender wage gap continues to widen up to the age of 42. During this time, those who can't work excessive hours could miss out on career opportunities.

Any kind of work flexibility can come at a high price in terms of career progression, as I found in my study of professional and managerial women's exit from work, conducted with organisational psychologist Emma Cahusac. We found that even women who continued to work full-time after having a child were disadvantaged because in professional and

managerial work, full time often means being available any time. Many women are pushed into less interesting work because face time and on-call availability are disproportionately rewarded.

Reducing women's domestic work can contribute to closing the gender pay gap. Numerous studies have shown that housework is negatively associated with wages. This is why it matters when men do much less around the home than women. Their contributions have gradually increased to a small degree, with men's involvement in childcare picking up more than their participation in the mundane daily housework tasks. But women still perform the lion's share, and tend to take responsibility for domestic work, taking on the 'mental load' of making sure chores get done.

Organisations reinforce this unequal sharing in the home when they make working long hours a pre-condition for success. Such company cultures uphold an unspoken 'gendered contract' that it is women who are meant to perform care.

Working fewer hours

If long hours are an ingredient of success in modern organisations, not everyone is convinced – even those who benefit. I conducted a study with University of Luxembourg sociologist Robin Samuel which showed that on average even male breadwinners – the main beneficiaries of the long hours system and those who actually work the longest hours – would prefer to work fewer hours for less pay. Further, when male breadwinners want to work fewer hours, our research shows it's often because they feel their jobs interfere with their family lives.

Recent examples of toxic workplaces should encourage debate about what it is reasonable to expect from employees. Gender inequalities relating to the reconciliation of work and care remain largely a side issue within organisations, although both the crisis of care and how people can accomplish work and care are critical issues facing our society. The #MeToo movement shone a light on sexual harassment, but it hasn't been the turning point many had hoped for in terms of boosting gender equality at work. There has been a substantial backlash to it, in part emanating from the gulf in understanding between those affected by such abuse and those who perpetrate or condone it.

A similar divergence can be seen in discussions about toxic workplaces – whether that's about bullying or deep-rooted employer expectations about working practices such as long hours, which systematically disadvantage some employees. Some people may see working long hours as linked to being robust, high-achieving, results-driven and demanding, others believe it diminishes employees and degrades the workplace environment.

28 April 2023

Debate

'Housewives and mothers should be paid for housework'.

Debate this motion as a class, with one group arguing in favour and one group arguing against.

THE CONVERSATION

The above information is reprinted with kind permission from The Conversation.
© 2010-2023, The Conversation Trust (UK) Limited

www.theconversation.com

Women's equality at risk of being put back 25 years by the pandemic

Currently at 15%, the gender gap still needs to be bridged, women's conference is told.

More than 50 years after the Equal Pay Act was passed, women at work and in retirement continue to face widespread discrimination – and the situation has worsened since the pandemic, UNISON's annual women's conference heard last week.

According to the Office of National Statistics, the gender pay gap currently stands at 15% for full-time workers and is much wider when employed part-time, as most women are.

Working years

Proposing a motion 'gender pay justice for women workers', Kate Ramsden of Scotland region told delegates: 'Workers – mainly women – stepped up during COVID to keep this country going. There was a recognition that these jobs were essential. Now – despite the clapping during COVID – we're back to business as usual.

'Women enter the labour force already disadvantaged because of our as roles as mothers and carers, and we pay the price. These are wonderful jobs, jobs that should be valued and respected and properly remunerated – but they're not.'

The UN's women's data report for 2020 has estimated that women's equality is at risk of being set back 25 years due to the pandemic. The UN has therefore reaffirmed its commitment to improving women's work conditions to combat this rollback.

Yet policymakers have turned their backs on the women workers who made up the majority of frontline workers during the pandemic, conference heard.

'We know that work done by women is neither valued nor paid its worth by society. In fact it is disgracefully underpaid, undervalued and precarious, and the situation is worsening,' stated Ms Ramsden. 'This means that women are now bearing the brunt of the cost of living crisis, struggling to feed themselves and their families and to keep their homes.'

In passing the motion, delegates called on the national women's committee to:

- Ensure meaningful actions to tackle gender pay gaps are included in future pay claims;

- Lobby UK governments to bring forward meaningful legislation to close the gaps, with penalties for employers who fail to do so.

Retirement

'Women are short-changed through their working lives and then through retirement,' Dawn Johnson, North Cumbria, Northumberland and Tyne & Wear health branch, told delegates.

'Women are much more likely to take maternity leave when they have a baby, so that lessens their pension. They're more likely to have caring responsibilities and work part time, that

lessens their pension. Low paid workers are largely women, that lessens their pension. Younger women are more likely to suffer from gender-related illnesses, like PMS [premenstrual syndrome] and these lessen their pension.'

Also women statistically struggle more following a divorce, which often leads to them withdrawing from pension schemes to make ends meet, she added. 'And that's all before we've reached the menopause. I know women who've taken early retirement due to the menopause. Again this affects their pensions.'

The TUC has calculated that the income gap between men and women in retirement is a massive 38%.

'I never expected to have to work until I was 66. I am a domiciliary care worker which is a very intense job,' said Pam McKenzie, Northern Ireland branch. 'I suffer from rheumatoid arthritis, as a result of my job, but I can't afford to retire. I took time out to have three children. I also had to reduce my hours because I have two elderly parents and a disabled grandchild. I have to work longer now to get a full pension.

'I have two brothers and they don't have to work longer. They think it's my job, they say it's women's work.'

Pauline Baker, Suffolk branch, added: ' I didn't take time out to have children and I've worked since I was 16, but I still don't know whether I'll be able to afford to live on the state pension. I have a mortgage, I've got heating costs and special dietary needs.'

Added to this, it came to light in July 2022, that due to errors made by the Department for Work and Pensions in national insurance credits, certain married women, widows and over 80s are owed around £1.5 million in back payments, which still hasn't been paid.

Rosie MacGregor, national retired members' committee, said: 'The income for women pensioners is hugely disproportionate to those of men – almost half the income, by many estimates. Tens of thousands of women have been underpaid their state pension and they're still having to wait many years for compensation – building injustice on injustice.'

Conference approved the motion on the gender pension gap, to:

- Work with UNISON's pension department to improve understanding of the current situation;

- Develop easy-to-understand information sheets about pensions, to be sent to all women members;

- Work with LAOS to provide training for women to help them improve their current pension outcomes;

- Work with Labour Link to lobby the government to lower the auto-enrolment threshold for state pensions, to support the union's lowest paid women and those with multiple low-paid jobs.

Fighting for fairness and equality

One of UNISON's main aims is to help workers fight for fairness and equality in the workplace and beyond. Challenging discrimination and winning equality is at the heart of everything UNISON does.

Equal pay

People doing the same job or work of equal value should get the same or equal pay; but in many cases they don't, even though the law says they should. UNISON actively campaigns for fair and equal pay.

20 February 2023

What is the 'pink tax' and how does it hinder women?

By Spencer Feingold, World Economic Forum

- **Gender-based price disparities are known as pink taxes.**

- **The pink tax has long imposed an economic burden on women – especially since women continue to earn less than men.**

- **The United Nations has called on countries to eliminate the pink tax to ensure women have full and equal access to economic participation.**

Men and women often buy similar day-to-day products. But research shows that consumer products targeted and advertised to women are sometimes more expensive than comparable products marketed to men. This disparity is referred to as a so-called pink tax.

Gender-based price disparities are prevalent in several sectors, but one of the most visible is personal care products. These include, for example, soaps, lotions, razor blades and deodorants that are marketed specifically to either women or men.

In the United States, one government study analysed 800 gender-specific products from nearly 100 brands. The report found that, on average, personal care products targeted to women were 13% more expensive than similar men's products. Accessories and adult clothing were 7% and 8% more expensive, respectively. The study concluded that 'women are paying thousands of dollars more over the course of their lives to purchase similar products as men.' Another US study found that dry cleaning prices for women's dress shirts were upwards of 90% more expensive than for men's shirts.

Meanwhile, an analysis in the UK found that women's deodorant was on average 8.9% more expensive than men's. Women's facial moisturiser was 34.28% more expensive.

The World Economic Forum's *Global Gender Gap Report 2022*, released this week, found that when it comes to wage equality for similar work, only five out of the 146 countries analysed achieved scores higher than 0.80. (A score of 1.0 would mean full wage parity.) Moreover, 129 countries this year reported a reduction of women's labour-force participation relative to men's. The gender pay gap, the report found, is one of the most salient factors contributing to the overall gender-based wealth inequality.

Efforts are underway to curb the pink tax. In fact, the United Nations has called on countries worldwide to take steps to eliminate the pink tax to ensure women achieve full and equal participation in the economy.

In the US, proposed federal legislation called the Pink Tax Repeal Act remains pending in the Congress. 'The pink tax is blatantly discriminatory, affecting women from all walks of life from the cradle to the grave,' Congresswoman Jackie Speier of California, the lead sponsor of the legislation, said in a statement.

As part of understanding the pink tax, researchers and policymakers also examine the imposed costs of products necessary for women to buy that are not necessary for men, like tampons.

Advocates have long worked to lower or eliminate taxes on tampons and other feminine sanitary products, recognizing the burden they place on women – especially those on lower-incomes. Several countries – including Australia, Canada, India, and Rwanda, among others – have eliminated taxes on tampons and other feminine products.

14 July 2022

www.weforum.org

The emptiness of International Women's Day

Against glass-ceiling feminism.

By Nina Welsch

Last month, I came across a video on Twitter. A minute long, it showed footage of a nine-year-old girl in Afghanistan being dragged away from her mother by the fifty-eight-year-old man she was being forced to marry. 'Don't you dare look away,' read one of the comments. I obeyed. The screams of both mother and daughter as they were pulled apart are still bothering me at night.

They are echoing in my mind today on International Women's Day, an annual celebration of the accomplishments of women in all corners of the globe and reflection on the oppression that remains. As a concept, it's rather ambitious in scope and often ends up a bit of mess tonally, with female leaders in politics and business paying lip service to the plight of abuse victims whilst simultaneously owning what #girlbosses they are. In the last few years, haunted by the spectre of gender identity, it's become even more broad and icky in its focus.

The theme for 2023 is #embraceequity, i.e. fairness, inclusivity. If you go to the official website, you are greeted by a series of photographs of people of all races and genders hugging themselves. 'All IWD activity is valid, that's what makes IWD inclusive.' So you say. In the one hundred or so articles you can read under their list of 'Missions' for this year, there are countless centred on empowerment, the workplace and technological innovation, a single one on a campaign to end slavery and absolutely nothing targeting violence against women. In a campaign so rabidly obsessed with inclusion, quite a pertinent issue has been excluded.

'This is not the language of activism; it is the language of utopia-think.'

'Imagine a gender equal world,' reads the homepage. 'A world free of bias, stereotypes, and discrimination. A world that's diverse, equitable, and inclusive. A world where difference is valued and celebrated. Together we can forge women's equality. Collectively we can all #EmbraceEquity.'

This is not the language of activism; it is the language of utopia-think, as betrayed by the very first word: 'Imagine'. There is a time and a place to dress for the job you want, not the job you have – or, in this case, design a campaign for the reality you wish existed as opposed to facing the grim realities that affect the most vulnerable. 'Everyone, everywhere can play a part', or so the website claims. I can think of a nine-year-old child bride who can't.

Lifelong women's rights campaigner Julie Bindel coined a marvellous phrase: 'glass-ceiling feminism'. Put simply, it is the feminist equivalent of trickle-down economics. It is the belief that equity for women at the top – the CEOs, the political leaders, the Professor Dames et al – will ultimately lead to justice for women 'in the basement' as Bindel would put it: those trapped and brutalised and enslaved. The idea that power begets empowerment arguably works for young, ambitious graduate women keen to climb a male-dominated career ladder. For an Afghani girl sold into a lifetime of unimaginable abuse though, her fundamental need is safety. Whilst I would never equate the oppression

Chapter 2: Obstacles to Equality

faced by women and girls under Taliban rule and whatever sex-based oppression exists in Britain, the reality is that for any woman who has been trapped due to male violence or sexual abuse, glass-ceiling feminism has no relevance. Since buddying up with an unexpected bedfellow – 'intersectional' feminism – it has become downright detrimental to them.

I won't go into the ideological intricacies of intersectional feminism (otherwise known as 'liberal feminism'), but one of its key values is that feminism is for everyone. It has designed itself as such, notably by disassociating womanhood from femaleness. The two things can overlap if you are a 'cis' woman, but to dare claim they are synonymous is to be a 'bio-essentialist', 'gender-Karen' or plain old TERF.

Intersectional feminism is not woman-centric, and neither is its leadership: Sadiq Khan, Owen Jones and Juno Dawson are the faces of it as much as Emma Watson or Nicola Sturgeon. That said, you can see the allure of it to young, aspirational women who fear the glass ceiling. If the possibility of pregnancy is what causes the barrier, removing all relevance of female biology from being a woman is theoretically beneficial. On top of that, the language of intersectional feminism – kindness, inclusivity, awareness of white privilege and cis privilege, pro-LGBTQ+, anti-racism and so forth – speaks to a sense of idealism in the young. It also speaks to a sense of liberal guilt to those privileged enough to be in the boardroom above the metaphorical ceiling.

'The product stinks, but the branding is very good.'

Unfortunately, glass can catch the light in a way that dazzles. Having been weaned on intersectional/glass-ceiling feminism myself at university, as a young, cripplingly insecure bookish girl reeling from a childhood mired in domestic violence, the pseudo-logic spoke to me. Unwavering support for the liberation of all – whatever their concerns or version of reality – will equate to liberation for women by default. For me. It is insidious individualism brilliantly marketed as inclusion. The product stinks, but the branding is very good, from its alluring slogans to the complimentary rainbow lanyards.

International Women's Day has evidently bought it. Let's face it, the feminism for which Julie Bindel and many members of the gender critical movement fight – what Bindel herself would call 'real' feminism – is a bloody hard sell. Whilst there's no denying many sexist stereotypes have been socially constructed throughout history and can to a point be dismantled (by men as well as women), it inconveniently points out that the female body, for all its child-growing wonders, comes with severe physical disadvantages. All female oppression stems from this. It brings to light the deeply harrowing realisation that, by virtue of our biology, our sex, all of us could have been that nine-year-old girl dragged from her mother. It dares you not to look away. Posing for a #embraceequity selfie feels vastly more empowering.

This is a tale of two feminisms. One will always win the argument, and one will nearly always win the ego. It's not that glass-ceiling feminism doesn't care about the plight of the genuinely marginalised; it just doesn't care enough to de-invest in its own crap. Whilst it can pay occasional token lip service to cultural atrocities committed against women across the globe, it can never go beyond this. Doing so would expose the disembodied theory it stands on as fragile and transparent. The pursuit of utopia is an excellent distraction from the hellish realities you are conveniently choosing not to look down at.

Its cleverest marketing strategy to date? Appropriating the word 'feminism' to make its brand the definitive one. One of many slogans often tweet-lectured at the likes of Julie Bindel is, 'If your feminism isn't intersectional, it isn't real feminism.' Quite a catch-22: feminism is for everyone – except the women's rights activists who dare highlight it can't possibly be for everyone whilst retaining meaning or focus. At this point, I'd almost suggest we surrender the label to them. I privately renounced it as part of my identity a while back, unable to bear any association. As much as some might despair at my defeatism, at the end of the day it's not words or hashtags that matter to abused women and girls. International Women's Day has forgotten this.

8 March 2023

'Motherhood penalty' leaves British gender equality worse than Poland and Hungary

Childcare costs put UK behind 13 other OECD countries for workplace equality.

By Eir Nolsøe

Britain has fallen behind Poland and Hungary in gender equality rankings as excessively high childcare costs keep women out of the workforce.

The UK now ranks 14th among 33 OECD countries for workplace equality, according to a new report from PwC.

Britain has fallen five places in the rankings over the last year, dropping behind Finland, Belgium, Ireland, Hungary and Poland.

PwC said rising childcare costs were keeping British mothers out of the workforce and holding back their lifetime career progression.

Nursery fees in Britain have risen by a fifth since 2017, significantly outpacing inflation. The availability of childcare providers has shrunk by 10% in the past four years.

Larice Stielow, senior economist at PwC, said: 'For many it is more affordable to leave work than remain in employment and pay for childcare, especially for families at lower income levels.'

PwC found the gender pay gap in the UK grew by 2.4 percentage points to 14.4%. Britain's increase was four times the OECD average.

Ms Stielow said: 'The motherhood penalty is now the most significant driver of the gender pay gap and, in the UK, women are being hit even harder by the rising cost of living and increasing cost of childcare.'

Parents in the UK contend with much higher childcare costs than other developed nations. British parents typically spend almost a third of their monthly income on childcare, compared to just 1% for German couples, PwC said.

Separate research published by the British Chamber of Commerce on Tuesday found that women were nearly twice as likely as men to say childcare responsibilities had hurt their career progression. Two thirds of mothers said caring duties had held them back, the BCC said.

Chancellor Jeremy Hunt is reportedly considering some giveaways for parents in next week's Budget in an effort to help more parents back to work and address large-scale labour shortages.

Businesses have urged the Chancellor to extend free childcare hours to parents with young children, however, the Treasury is understood to believe this would be too expensive.

Luxembourg, New Zealand and Slovenia scored highest in terms of gender equality, PwC said. The auditor looked at a range of metrics such as female labour force participation, unemployment and pay gap.

Tackling the root of the gender pay gap problem would require addressing parental leave, the report said.

Zlatina Loudjeva, partner in PwC's International Development team, said: 'We should consider enhanced parental leave policies and more flexible working so that all parents can balance work and caring responsibilities, alongside tackling the cost of childcare.'

Closing the gender pay gap across the OECD would take 50 years with the current pace of change, PwC said.

7 March 2023

How the 'chore gap' is still holding female founders back

By Aria Babu

I live in a bubble. To me, the idea that there are, in 2022, couples that aren't splitting their chores evenly, seems alien to me. But the data shows how naïve I am.

In opposite-sex couples in the UK, where the woman works full time 39% of them say they split their chores evenly and 38% say the woman does the majority of the housework. Only 9% of men who work full-time are responsible for the majority of housework.

Yesterday, we at The Entrepreneurs Network released a new report with Barclays about female founders and the extra barriers they face. We surveyed women who founded successful, high-growth businesses (defined here as businesses that have raised at least £1 million of equity finance). We found that despite being incredibly successful professionally, female entrepreneurs who live with romantic partners take on about the same amount of housework as other working women, with 44% saying they split their chores evenly and 38% saying they do the majority.

But, this surface-level data obscures part of the story. The chore gap widens after couples have children. When you break down the data further into founders who are mothers and founders who are not parents, you see that founders without children are much more likely to split their chores evenly, but half of founders with children say that they do the majority of the housework.

Considering the fact that having children means that the amount of housework in a home increases and that the majority of this increased housework goes to the mother, it is no surprise then that the female founders in our sample are less likely to have children than the general population. From the ages of our sample, you would expect about 69% to be mothers, instead 53% are.

When talking to our female founders, one of the main barriers to female entrepreneurship, expressed time and time again, is a lack of access to childcare.

As childcare continues to get more expensive, more and more women are locked out of the workforce. According to a recent survey from Pregnant Then Screwed, the financial burden of childcare has meant that 17% of parents have had to leave their jobs, with 62% saying they work fewer hours because of childcare costs.

I've written before for CapX about ways we can make childcare cheaper. The Government should treat the cost of childcare as a priority and there are a lot of options available to them.

Unless they do so, more and more women are going to be locked out of either motherhood or professional success.

The promise of 21st century feminism was that we could have it all, and when we look to other nations, or even our recent past, this seems to have been the case. But excessive regulation, inflexible subsidy options, and planning are driving costs up and pushing women out of the workforce.

The barriers faced by female founders are the same as the barriers faced by all women with careers that they value. After the high cost of childcare, female founders talked about facing discrimination at work and lacking the same networks that men have. Childcare and household labour is just one part of the puzzle, but without it we won't see true equality in any part of the labour force.

29 November 2022

Key Fact

- In opposite-sex couples in the UK, where the woman works full time 39% say they split their chores evenly and 38% say the woman does the majority of the housework.

Girls worldwide lag behind boys in mathematics, failed by discrimination and gender stereotypes – UNICEF

Girls worldwide are lagging behind boys in mathematics, with sexism and gender stereotypes among the root causes, according to a new report published today by UNICEF.

Solving the equation: Helping girls and boys learn mathematics features new data analyses covering more than 100 countries and territories. The report finds that boys have up to 1.3 times the odds of obtaining mathematics skills than girls. Negative gender norms and stereotypes often held by teachers, parents, and peers regarding girls' innate inability to understand mathematics are contributing to the disparity. This also undermines girls' self-confidence, setting them up for failure, the report notes.

'Girls have an equal ability to learn mathematics as boys – what they lack is an equal opportunity to acquire these critical skills,' said UNICEF Executive Director Catherine Russell. 'We need to dispel the gender stereotypes and norms that hold girls back – and do more to help every child learn the foundational skills they need to succeed in school and in life.'

Learning mathematics skills in turn strengthens memory, comprehension, and analysis, in turn improving children's ability to create, the report notes. Ahead of next week's United Nations Transforming Education Summit, UNICEF warns that children who do not master basic mathematics and other foundational learning may struggle to perform critical tasks such as problem solving and logical reasoning.

An analysis of data from 34 low- and middle-income countries featured in the report shows that while girls lag behind boys, three-quarters of schoolchildren in grade 4 are not obtaining foundational numeracy skills. Data from 79 middle- and high-income countries show more than a third of 15-year-old schoolchildren have yet to achieve minimum proficiency in mathematics.

Household wealth is also a determining factor. The report notes that schoolchildren from the richest households have 1.8 times the odds of acquiring numeracy skills by the time they reach fourth grade than children from the poorest households. Children who attend early childhood education and care programmes have up to 2.8 times the odds of achieving minimum proficiency in mathematics by the age of 15 than those who do not.

The report also notes the impact of the COVID-19 pandemic has likely further exacerbated children's mathematics abilities. Moreover, these analyses focus on girls and boys who are currently in school. In countries where girls are more likely to be out of school than boys, the overall disparities in mathematics proficiency are most likely even wider.

UNICEF is calling on governments to commit to reaching all children with quality education. We are urging new effort and investment to re-enrol and retain all children in school, to increase access to remedial and catchup learning, to support teachers and give them the tools they need, and to make sure that schools provide a safe and supportive environment so all children are ready to learn.

'With the learning of an entire generation of children at risk, this is not the time for empty promises. To transform education for every child, we need action and we need it now,' said Russell.

14 September 2022

Two in five Britons think championing women's equality discriminates against men

The recent rise of misogynistic views pushed by the likes of influencer Andrew Tate demonstrate the battle to achieve gender equality is far from over, campaigners say.

By Maya Oppenheim, Women's Correspondent

Two in five Britons think efforts to champion women's equality are so robust that men are being discriminated against, a major new study has suggested.

The research, carried out by King's College London and Ipsos, found that 53 per cent of men back that view while a third of women take the viewpoint.

The study, shared exclusively with *The Independent* to mark International Women's Day, discovered 38 per cent of respondents think there has been enough progress in giving women equal rights to their male counterparts. This marks a substantial jump of 13 percentage points since 2018 – with a quarter of people holding this view then.

Researchers who polled over 22,000 adults in 32 countries, also found that 38 per cent think men are being asked to do too much to champion equality, a substantial rise from the 29 per cent who held this view in 2019.

Julia Gillard, chair of the Global Institute for Women's Leadership at King's College London, said: 'Despite the progress, we've made in recent decades, high-profile examples of misogyny are still rife, particularly online, and there are worrying signs from this research that such views are not only gaining ground among the public, but also deterring people from advocating for women's rights.'

The study discovered the proportion of Britons who say they are frightened to champion the equal rights of women in case they face reprisals has doubled since 2017 – up from 14 per cent to 29 per cent.

Similar trends were identified around the world – with a global average of 37 per cent saying they are scared to speak out.

Ms Gillard, who was Australia's prime minister between 2010 and 2013, noted the researchers discovered that younger generations in the UK were the most likely to believe a man who 'stays home' to do childcare is 'less of a man'. This is a 'disturbing reminder there is still much more to do, and that future progress is not guaranteed', she warned.

She added: 'We can't be sure if these trends are the direct result of certain individuals gaining greater attention for their extreme and misogynistic views, but with reports of teachers and parents fearing that young people – and particularly young boys – are buying into a sexist ideology because of what they hear and read online, it's a question that urgently requires more research.

'And it's something that tallies with our findings, with the youngest surveyed sometimes the most likely to hold sexist views. Also worthy of more investigation is whether we're seeing a broader backlash to gender equality post-#MeToo, which could be contributing to these shifts in attitudes.'

Ms Gillard, Australia's only female PM, warned there were indications this is occurring given the extent of 'vitriol' directed at women in the spotlight such as Scotland's first minister Nicola Sturgeon and former New Zealand prime minister Jacinda Ardern, who both cited abuse and intimidation as factors behind their resignations.

'It's up to all of us to protect the rights we have won and to keep the fire of progress burning.' – Mandu Reid

'It's this feature of our life online that risks jeopardising progress on gender equality, and one we must guard against,' she said.

Mandu Reid, leader of the Women's Equality Party, said the research findings were 'alarming' and demonstrated the battle to achieve gender equality is 'far from over'.

She added: 'The rise of the far right has made misogynistic views more mainstream. You see the likes of Andrew Tate. They become a magnet for people who are unsettled by the progress women and marginalised groups have made.

'Our opposition have spokespeople like Jair Bolsonaro who are charismatic who can inspire those who feel afraid and undermined. These statistics show they are having an impact on people.'

Mr Tate is a former kickboxing world champion-turned-influencer now famed for his misogynistic views. The Independent previously reported on research by the Centre for Countering Digital Hate (CCDH) which unearthed 47 videos of Mr Tate pushing what it describes as 'extreme misogyny'.

While Mr Bolsonaro is Brazil's former far-right, populist president who publicly abused a female lawmaker, shoving her and telling her she was 'too ugly to deserve rape'.

However, Ms Reid said that the 'movement for equality is powerful' and was paving the way for change 'slowly but surely'.

'This resistance proves it. It's up to all of us to protect the rights we have won and to keep the fire of progress burning,' she added.

8 March 2023

A climate crisis is becoming a crisis for gender equality

Sian Norris reports how news that East Africa's drought is entering its fifth year spells danger for women and girls.

By Sian Norris, Chief Social and European Affairs Reporter

Byline Times revealed today that the rainy season in East Africa is set to fail for the fifth year in a row, as the 62nd Greater Horn of Africa Climate Outlook Forum confirmed that the rains may not come this year. Speaking at a press conference in Mombasa, the representatives confirmed predictions made in May, including by the UK Met Office, that the rains would continue to fail.

Already, more than 16 million people in the Greater Horn cannot access enough water for drinking, cooking and cleaning. The drought has caused widespread displacement, malnutrition and death in Kenya, Somalia and Ethiopia. The latter two countries continue to struggle with violent conflict.

Sadia Allin, Plan International's head of mission in Somalia and Somaliland, told Byline Times: 'East Africa is in the grip of its worst drought in decades. In Somalia, we're seeing extreme, widespread hunger, with parts of the country at risk of famine. The reality is that children are dying, and loss of life on a devastating scale is now a very real risk'.

For women and girls, this food crisis has become a crisis of equality. Gender stereotypes mean that men are prioritised when it comes to food and meal times, with girls given smaller portions or not fed at all. Little wonder, then, that women and girls make up 70% of the world's hungry. At the same time, food insecurity leads to girls being married off at younger and younger ages, to relieve the financial burden on their families.

When livestock dies and crops fail, families are plunged into deepening poverty. They may no longer be able to afford school fees, textbooks and uniforms. The number of children at risk of dropping out of school in Ethiopia, Kenya and Somalia due to the impact of the drought trebled between March and June this year – from 1.1 million to an estimated 3.3 million children, with girls disproportionately likely to leave the classroom.

Often when this happens, girls are required to help out with household chores or to care for younger siblings so their parents can find work. Some children will be sent out to work themselves in order to bring in extra income.

But in the most extreme cases, girls who have left the classroom are married off when still children themselves, becoming trapped in a lifetime of pregnancy, childbirth and gender-based violence.

It's for this reason that the United Nations' children and families agency Unicef has warned that the region's most severe drought in 40 years is leading to 'alarming' rates of forced early marriage and female genital mutilation (FGM). In Ethiopia, one of the worst impacted countries, child marriage rates are estimated to have more than doubled over the past year.

This is particularly devastating when for years, there has been real progress in eradicating FGM – a form of child abuse that involves cutting or removing the clitoris and some of the labia. Now Unicef data warns the practice is on the rise: in the Southern Nations, Nationalities, and Peoples' Region in the Horn of Africa, it's estimated that cases of FGM rose by 27%.

The cycle of violence

Girls who are married off as children are at risk of rape and further gender-based violence. They become mothers when they are still children themselves. And the loss of schooling means they often struggle to gain financial independence when they are older.

'At Plan International, we're especially worried about the impact on girls,' said Allin. 'When food is scarce, girls often eat least and last, or simply go without. On top of that, when families are under financial strain, girls are at greater risk of gender-based violence and early marriage as parents marry off their girls in exchange for assistance. For many, the chance for an education will be lost forever'.

In some parts of Somalia, there has been a 50% rise in gender-based violence, including domestic abuse and child marriage, according to a Unicef survey. In Puntland, a northwestern state in Somalia, service providers told Unicef that child marriage made up 59% of the cases they were dealing with, many of which involved FGM.

Child marriage rates often correlate with increased incidents of FGM, as girls are cut in preparation for getting married. A total of 14 out of the 23 countries affected by the drought are FGM hotspots, with prevalence rates of up to 98%. FGM is a form of gender-based child abuse, with cut girls experiencing a range of long-term health impacts, including trauma, difficulties with menstruation, and pregnancy complications.

Further, women and girls are more vulnerable to sexual violence and intimate partner violence during drought. It tends to be women and girls who are responsible for collecting water – but with water in scarce supply, they are having to make longer and more dangerous journeys. Kenya Red Cross has estimated women and girls are walking more than three times longer than before, up to 30km in some locations, to get water. The walk is fraught with danger, including the potential risk of rape.

Research published in 2020 found that drought in sub-Saharan Africa was associated with reporting a controlling partner and experiencing physical and sexual violence, with stronger associations among adolescent girls and unemployed women.

'Right now, Plan International is trucking water to drought affected communities and providing emergency cash to help families struggling with severe food shortages,' said Allin. 'We're also rapidly scaling up our programmes, with added support for child protection and girls' education. But we urgently need more funds. We have a window of opportunity to act, and we urge the UK public to give what they can'.

26 August 2022

Further Reading/ Useful Websites

Useful Websites

www.bylinetimes.com

www.capx.co

www.fawcettsociety.org.uk

www.ifs.org.uk

www.independent.co.uk

www.ipsos.com

www.iqeq.com

www.kcl.ac.uk

www.lordslibrary.parliament.uk

www.mintel.com

www.openaccessgovernment.org

www.telegraph.co.uk

www.theconversation.com

www.thecritic.co.uk

www.theguardian.com

www.unicef.org.uk

www.unison.org.uk

www.weforum.org

Further reading/References

Page 1: Global Gender Gap Report 2022 - World Economic Forum, The Motherhood Penalty by Joelie Brearley

Page 7:International Women's Day, 'About International Women's Day 2023', accessed 27 February 2023

Office for National Statistics, 'Gender pay gap in the UK: 2022', 26 October 2022 House of Lords Library, 'Status of women and girls in the UK since 2010', 7 July 2022

Page 8: Fawcett's 2022 Sex & Power Index: www.fawcettsociety.org.uk/sex-power-2022

Pages 12-13: Andrew, A., Bandiera, O., Costa-Dias, M. and Landais, C. (2021), 'Women and men at work', IFS Deaton Review of Inequalities, https://ifs.org.uk/inequality/women-and-men- at-work

Page 17: Women in the Workplace 2020 Report (McKinsey)

Pages 16-18: Naumann, I. et al (2022): 'Child and Parental Wellbeing during the Covid-Pandemic', Working Paper 1, 2022, UKRI Covid-19 rapid response project Childcare and Wellbeing in Times of Covid-19

Seedat, S. & Ronda, M. (2021): 'Women's wellbeing and the burden of unpaid work', BMJ 2021; 374: n1972

OECD 2020: 'Is Childcare Affordable?', Policy Brief on Employment, Labour and Social Affairs, June 2020.

Coram Family and Childcare, Childcare Survey 2023

Pages 20-23: https://www.ipsos.com/en-uk/international-womens-day-global-opinion-remains-committed-to-gender-equality

Page 28: 'Unsuitable For Females: The Rise Of The Lionesses And Women's Football In England' by Carrie Dunn

Glossary

Chore gap

The chore gap is the term used to describe the inequality in how housework is divided between women and men.

Discrimination

Unfair treatment of someone because of the group/class they belong to.

Domestic labour

Work which takes place in the home: for example, minding children, cooking, cleaning.

Equality

The right of different groups of people to have a similar position, and/or receive the same treatment.

Equality Act 2010

This Act brings a number of existing laws together in one place. It sets out the personal characteristics that are protected by law, and behaviour which is unlawful. The 'protected characteristics' are age; disability; gender reassignment; marriage and civil partnership; pregnancy and maternity; race; religion and belief; sex and sexual orientation. Under the Act people are not allowed to discriminate against, harass or victimise another person because they have any of the protected characteristics.

Equity

When people are treated fairly according to their needs and no group of people are given special treatment.

Female genital mutilation (FGM)

FGM is a non-medical cultural practice that involves partially or totally removing a girl or woman's external genitalia.

Female infanticide

Infanticide is the unlawful killing of very young children and babies. Female infanticide specifically refers to the practice of killing female babies and young girls and is a practice that has been reported in India, China and parts of Africa, Asia and the Middle East.

Feminism

Advocating women's rights and equality between the sexes.

Gender

Gender refers to socially constructed roles, learned behaviours and expectations associated with females and males. Gender is more than just biology: it is the understanding we gain from society and those around us of what it means to be a girl/woman or a boy/man.

Gender bias

A preference or prejudice toward one gender over the other. Can be conscious or unconscious.

Gender neutral

A term not referring to either sex but referring to people in general.

Gender pay gap

At EU level, the gender pay gap is defined as the relative difference in the average gross hourly earnings of women and men within the economy as a whole. Currently, women earn on average 21% less than their male counterparts.

Gender quotas

A statement that an organisation or body must employ a minimum number of employees from a certain gender, in order to address a lack of male or female representation.

Gender stereotypes

Simplifying the roles, attributes and differences between males and females. Gender stereotyping encourages children to behave in ways that are considered most typical of their sex. For example, buying pink toys for girls and blue for boys, or limiting girls to playing with dolls and boys to toy-cars.

Glass ceiling

The term 'glass ceiling' refers to the problem of an invisible 'barrier' that prevents someone from progressing in their career to upper-level positions. Particularly for women and minorities.

International Women's Day (IWD)

International Women's Day is a global day celebrating the social, economic, cultural, and political achievements of women. IWD also raises awareness of discrimination and abuse against women and girls. IWD takes place annually on 8 March.

Pink tax

The term 'pink tax' refers to the extra money women are charged for certain products or services above the standard cost for comparable goods aimed at men; often these items are coloured pink to indicate they have been developed for female consumers.

Index

A
action, taking 22–23, 26, 34–35
Africa, East 40–41
age, and attitudes to equality 22–23, 24, 25–26

B
bias, unconscious 11
brands, and demands for equality 14–15

C
childcare 16–18, 30, 36, 37
climate crisis 40–41
consumers, influence of 14–15
Covid-19 pandemic 9, 14, 16, 31–32

D
developing countries 6–7, 10, 40–41
digital gender gap 4
diversity, equality and inclusion (DEI) initiatives 11
drought in East Africa 40–41

E
earnings 5, 11
economic participation and opportunity 2, 4, 5, 11
education 2, 4, 5–7, 12, 38
equity 11
ethnicity pay gap 8–9

F
fear of speaking out 22–23, 24, 39
female genital mutilation (FGM) 40–41
feminism 22, 25, 26, 34–35
Finland 2
flexible working 11, 29–30
football 27–28

G
Germany 3
glass-ceiling feminism 34–35
Global Gender Gap Report 2022 1–3, 4
government policies 5, 6–7, 10

H
health 2, 4, 5, 9
housework 13, 30, 37

I
Iceland 2
International Women's Day (IWD) 4, 34–35
intersectional feminism 34–35
Ireland 3

L
leadership roles 8–9, 11

M
marriage, forced 40–41
mathematics 38
men
    and childcare 16–17
    views on equality 20–21, 23, 25, 39
misogyny 26, 39

N
Namibia 3
New Zealand 2, 19
Nicaragua 3
Norway 2

O
overseas aid 6–7, 10

P
parenthood 13, 16–18, 29–30, 36
pay gap 8–9, 12, 14, 27–28, 29–30, 36
pensions 31–32
pink taxes 33
politics, women in 2–3, 4, 5, 9, 19, 39
products aimed at women 33

R
Rwanda 3

S
sexism 21–22, 25, 26
sport 8, 15, 27–28
STEM subjects 5–6, 38
survival 2
Sweden 3

U
United Nations (UN) 4

V
violence against women 40–41

W
women of colour 8–9
work
    paid 8–9, 11, 12–13, 29–30
    unpaid 13, 16–18, 30, 37
working hours 29–30
world rankings 1–3